HORSE OWNER'S HANDBOOK

Lloyd S. McKibbin, D.V.M.

Wheatley Hall Farm
Wheatley, Ontario
Canada

In collaboration with

Al Sugerman

Windfall Quarter Horse Farm
West Lorne, Ontario
Canada

W. B. SAUNDERS COMPANY
Philadelphia, London, Toronto

W. B. Saunders Company: West Washington Square
Philadelphia, PA 19105

1 St. Anne's Road
Eastbourne, East Sussex BN21 3UN, England

1 Goldthorne Avenue
Toronto, Ontario M8Z 5T9, Canada

Library of Congress Cataloging in Publication Data

McKibbin, Lloyd S

Horse owner's handbook.

1. Horses — Diseases.   I. Sugerman, Al, joint author.
   II. Title.

SF951.M23   636.1'08'9   75–44652

ISBN 0-7216-5920-9

Cover illustration courtesy of the American Quarter Horse Association, Amarillo, Texas.

Horse Owner's Handbook   ISBN 0-7216-5920-9

Last digit is the print number: 9   8   7   6   5   4   3   2

DEDICATION

This book is dedicated to my wife Connie, my
family, and my parents, as well as to the horses
and friends I have known and admired over the
many long years.

Biographical Notes

Dr. L.S. McKibbin was born in Ingersol, Ontario. He served in the Royal Canadian Air Force during the Second World War. After graduating from the Ontario Veterinary College, he decided to specialize in horses, and today he has one of the most successful equine practices in North America.

Dr. McKibbin has owned and raced several Thoroughbred and standardbred horses. Best known as Willy Tass, a trotter that finished in the money 134 times out of 300 starts.

Dr. McKibbin has pioneered several surgical and clinical techniques. He is a member of the Ontario Veterinary Society, the American Veterinary Medical Association, the British Equine Veterinary Association, the American Veterinary Radiology Society, the Canadian Veterinary Association, and the International Veterinary Acupuncture Society.

PHOTOGRAPHY
A. G. Sugerman

PREFACE

The purpose of this book is to create a closer understanding between the horse owner and the veterinarian. It is my purpose not to make a veterinarian out of a horseman but simply to increase the horseman's knowledge of his animal.

I have stressed principles of treatment rather than techniques. However, the techniques that are included in this book have been well tested over the years, and their success is documented in the daily newspaper and in the Racing Form, especially in the win, place, and show columns.

The photographs were taken from my personal files, which I have gathered over the past 20 years.

Many of my techniques were learned from my colleagues in the American Equine Practitioner's Association, British Veterinarian Equine Association, American Veterinary Radiology Society, Ontario Veterinary Association, American Veterinary Medical Association, and the Michigan Veterinary Medical Association. In this regard I would especially like to mention Dr. Dan Roberts, Wichita Falls, Texas; Dr. Alex Harthill, Louisville, Kentucky; Dr. James O'Connor, Epping, New Hampshire; Dr. James Roberts, Newmarket, England; and Dr. Edouard Pouret, Orne, France.

I would like to thank Dr. Robert Ordidge, my associate, for his article on pedal ostitis, and Dr. Ken Armstrong for his early work in aiding me in the use of Vitallium screwnails in orthopedic surgery.

I would also like to give special thanks to many friends in the medical profession who have conveyed to me many of their experiences, and to my clients who supplied me with a multitude of patients. I also want to mention my staff, who daily care for the more than 50 patients under their control; Miss Judy Vandenbrande, my anesthetist; and Al Sugerman for his assistance in helping me prepare this book.

L. S. McKibbin

CONTENTS

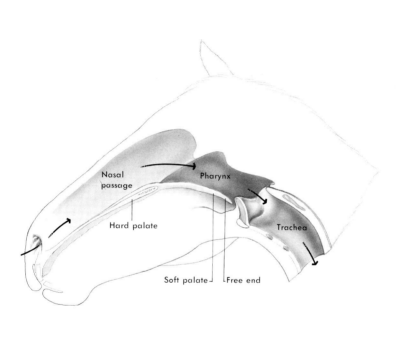

Nasal
passage

Pharynx

Hard palate

Trachea

Soft palate   Free end

HEAD, MOUTH, AND TEETH

DETERMINING THE AGE OF THE HORSE

Race horses are identified by tattoos on their upper lip. These horses also have registration papers, making their age easy to determine. However, thousands of horses, especially those in the pleasure horse industry, do not have this kind of refined identification. For this animal, therefore, it is necessary that the buyer be able to identify the age of the horse by his teeth.

Yearling Mouth

Figure 1 shows a full mouth of baby, or milk, teeth. The central incisors appear shortly after birth, but some colts may be born with these teeth. The next pair to appear, the lateral incisors, cut at four to six weeks. The corner incisors appear at six to nine months of age. These teeth are retained until the age of 2½ years. Baby or milk teeth are smooth and without the grooves that characterize permanent teeth.

Note in Figure 2 the dark line (*arrow*) that exists in front of the cup on the milk, or baby, teeth.

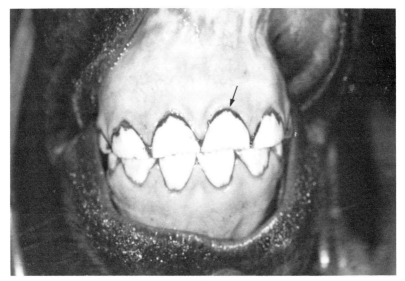

Figure 1

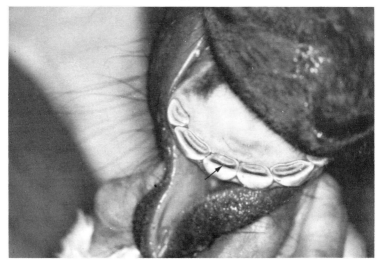

Figure 2

Age 2½ Years

By 2½ years of age the central incisor baby teeth have been shed, and the permanent teeth are coming in. The permanent teeth are longer and have grooves (Fig. 3).

Note in Figure 4 the cups or indentations (*arrows*) on the table surface of the permanent teeth. As the horse gets older these cups wear out.

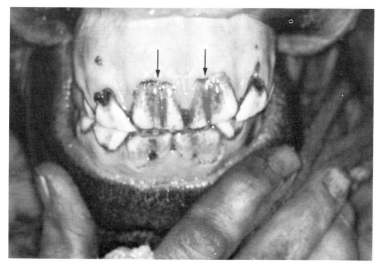

Figure 3

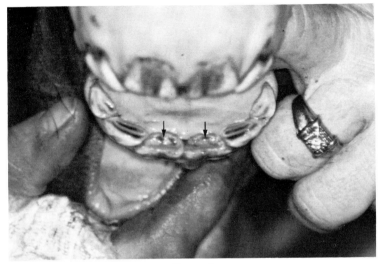

Figure 4

Age 3½ Years

At 3½ years of age both borders of the permanent central incisors (bottom) are in wear (C) and the lateral milk teeth are being shed (Fig. 5). A indicates where the baby tooth has been shed; and B is the baby tooth about to be shed.

Age 4½ Years

At 4½ years of age the corner baby teeth are being shed (B) and the permanent incisor is erupting. At this point the baby tooth must be removed manually to make room for the permanent tooth (Fig. 6).

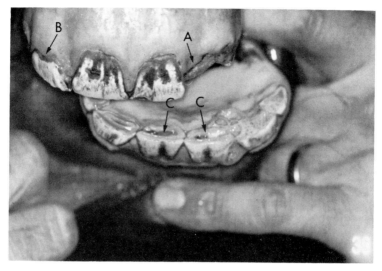

Figure 5

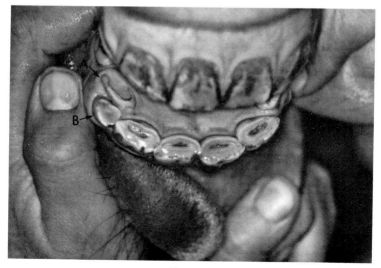

Figure 6

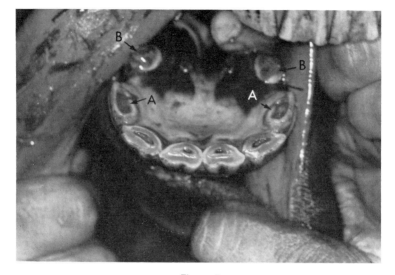

Figure 7

Age 5 Years

At 5 years of age the corner incisors are in full view; however, the back border behind the cup is not in wear (A). The horse now has a full set of teeth. Note in Figure 7 that the canines, or tushes (B), behind the corner incisors have erupted.

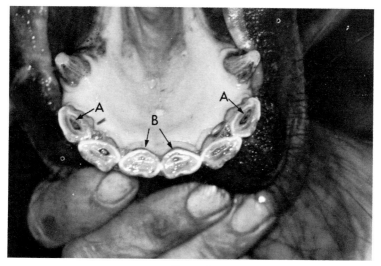

Figure 8

Age 6 Years

At 6 years of age the back border of the cup on the corner incisor (A) is in wear and the cup of the central incisor (B) is almost worn out (Fig. 8). In other words, it takes about 3½ years for a cup to wear out.

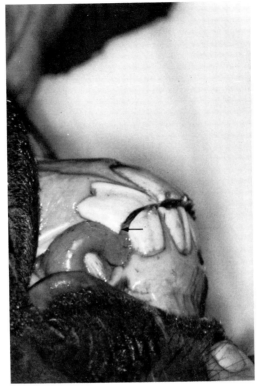

Figure 9

Age 7 Years

At 7 years of age the corner incisor has a slight hook, known as the *7-year hook* (Fig. 9). This is seen only when both the top and bottom jaws match.

Note in Figure 10 that the cup on the lateral incisor has worn out. (Remember that it takes 3½ years for a cup to wear out.) The tooth erupted at age 3½; therefore, this horse is 7 years old.

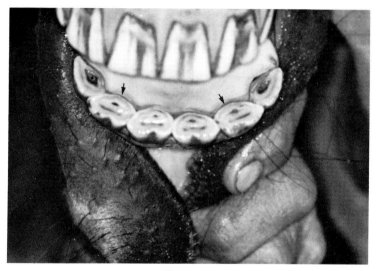

Figure 10

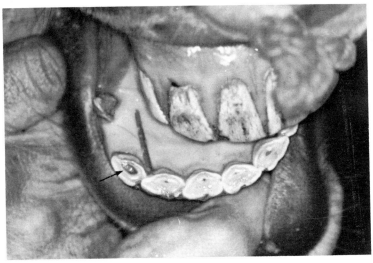

Figure 11

Age 8 Years

At 8 years of age the cup on the corner incisor is shallow, and the cups on the central and lateral incisors have disappeared (Fig. 11). The central incisors are becoming triangular in shape. They are the same distance from side to side as they are from front to back.

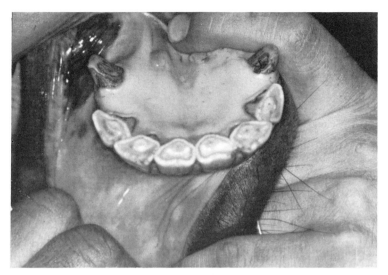

Figure 12

Age 9 Years

At 9 years of age the cups have disappeared in all six incisors. The lateral incisors have become triangular in shape, and the central incisors have begun to take on a circular shape (Fig. 12).

The upper corner incisor has started to develop what is known as *Galvayne's groove* (*arrow*) near the gum line (Fig. 13). At 15 years of age this groove extends halfway down the tooth. At 20 it reaches the bottom of the tooth and starts to disappear at the top. By the time the horse is 30 the groove will have disappeared. Figure 13 shows that at 9 years of age the teeth are starting to protrude forward, or become bucked.

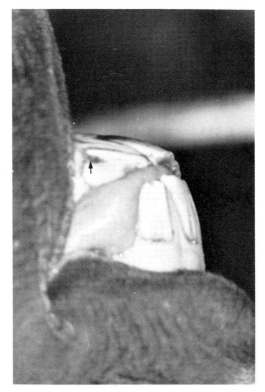

Figure 13

Age 12 to 14 Years

From 12 to 14 years of age all the teeth are round in appearance. The cups have disappeared, and the teeth are becoming smaller (Fig. 14). At this age the *Galvayne's groove* on the upper corner incisor is approaching the center of the tooth (*A*). Because the horse shown in Figure 15 is *parrot-mouthed* (has an overshot jaw) (*B*), the 7-year hook is missing (*C*).

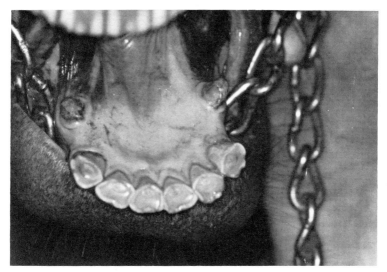

Figure 14

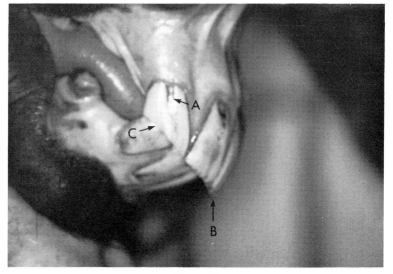

Figure 15

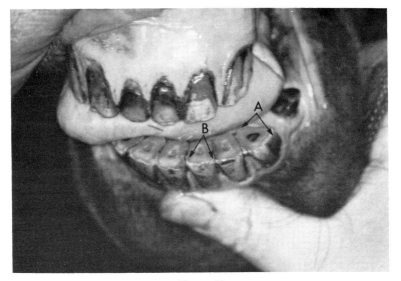

Figure 16

Age 20 Years

At 20 years of age the grinding surfaces of the teeth are much longer from front to back (A) than they are from side to side (B). In addition, the teeth have become much shorter (Fig. 16).

CAPS (BABY TEETH)

The 2½-year-old horse starts to shed his first premolar at the same time he is shedding his central incisors. Figure 17 shows the new tooth coming in (*arrow*). When the animal is 3 years old he starts to lose his upper and lower second premolars. These teeth should be extracted at this time to allow the new tooth to grow in straight.

Figure 18, an x-ray of the lower jaw, shows the position of the caps (baby teeth) on top of the permanent premolars, which are now emerging (*top arrows*). The bottom arrow indicates an abscess.

Figure 19 of a skull shows the baby premolar (*1*) sitting on top of the permanent premolar (*2*). When the horse is 4½ years of age, the third baby premolar (cap) comes off.

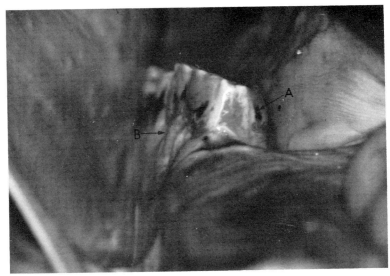

Figure 17

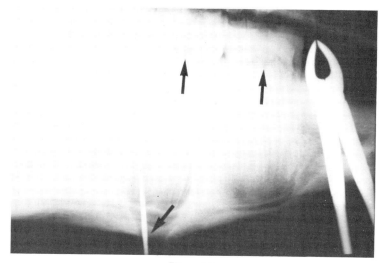

Figure 18

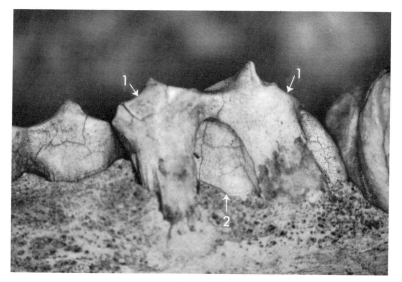

Figure 19

TARTAR

Tartar, although usually not a problem, can sometimes produce inflammation of the gums (Fig. 20) If inflammation does occur, the tartar should be removed with a small chisel.

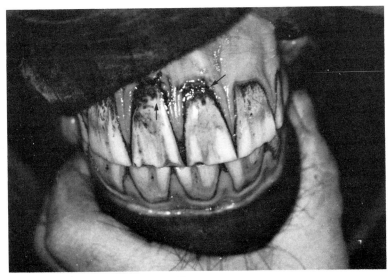

Figure 20

FLOATING

The term *floating* means filing the sharp points off the teeth. Points on the bottom jaw are on the inside, or tongue edge (Fig. 21), and points on the top jaw are on the cheek side (Fig. 22). This may be necessary if the horse cannot chew properly. Improper chewing should be suspected if whole oats can be seen in the horse's stool or if the animal drops an excessive amount of grain out of his mouth while eating.

Floating the teeth of a 2½-year-old is precarious, because if too much is taken off the corner of a colt's teeth, he can no longer chew his grain properly.

If a 3-year-old's teeth need floating, caps should be removed before the teeth are filed, since it is probable that the caps are naturally ready to come off at this time. Early in the 3-year-old the first upper and first lower premolar caps should be removed, and in the late 3-year-old the second upper and lower premolar caps should be ready to come off.

The same principle applies to a 4-year-old. His caps should be removed before his teeth are filed. However, if the caps are not ready to come off, then both the caps and the teeth must be floated.

A horse between the ages of 5 and 14 should have his teeth floated every six months. However, as the animal gets older, and especially after 20 years of age, floating should be done very carefully because the remaining part of the tooth could be knocked out of the animal's mouth. Special care should be taken that only the points, and not the grinding surfaces, are removed from the teeth.

Figure 23 shows the straight float, which is used on the bottom jaw, and the curved float, which is used on the top jaw.

The floats should be kept clean so that no disease is spread from one horse to another.

Figure 21

Figure 22

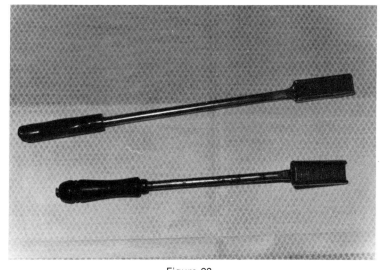

Figure 23

ABSCESSED OR SPLIT TOOTH

The horse that tends to chew his feed and then spit it out, so that the sides of his stall are covered with finely chewed hay, is probably suffering from an abscessed or a split tooth. Other symptoms include putrid breath and not taking the bit correctly.

An abscessed or split tooth is most likely to involve the third molar or cheek tooth in either the top or bottom jaw. In Figure 24, a Canadian quarter, which is the same size as an American quarter, has been placed next to an extracted molar to give the relative size of this tooth. Figure 25 shows an abscess on the bottom jaw that is a result of an abscessed premolar. Figure 26 indicates an abscess of a bottom premolar (arrows). A hole must be drilled through the lower jaw to facilitate removal of this tooth. These abscesses probably occur most frequently because the 4-year-old cap was not removed, and, as a result, food particles worked up the side of the tooth, causing decay.

An infected premolar that has caused ulceration of the gum is shown in Figure 27. The horse would not take the bit properly. Figure 28 indicates the location of the abscess. The arrow points to the probe in the center of the abscess.

Figure 24

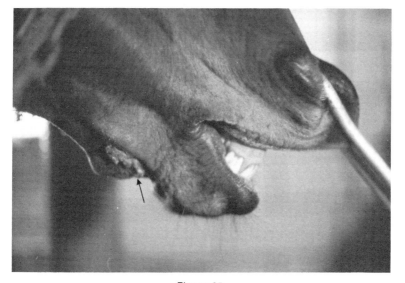

Figure 25

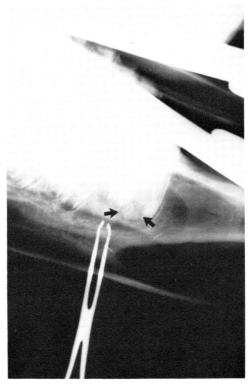

Figure 26

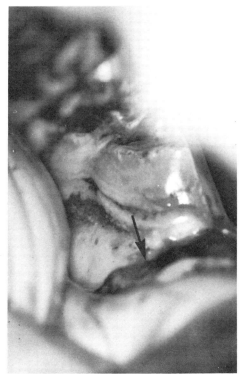

Figure 27

Treatment of an abscessed tooth requires removal of the tooth. If the involved tooth is in the bottom jaw, this is done by drilling a hole in the jaw bone and forcing the tooth out. If an upper tooth is infected, a hole is drilled through the skull immediately above the root (Fig. 29). An instrument called a "trephine" is used to drill this hole. This procedure establishes drainage, and the infection will clear up. Since horses have large, deeply embedded teeth, the tooth must be approached from the root in order to remove it.

The animal must be put under a general anesthetic. An elliptical incision is made over the root of the tooth, and the subcutaneous tissue is peeled back. A hole is drilled through the jaw bone. Removing the tooth generally requires two people. One person inserts a punch into the hole in the jaw bone (or skull) and tries to knock the tooth into the mouth. The assistant, using a large pair of forceps, slowly twists back and forth on the tooth until a suction sound is heard. This sound indicates that the tooth is loosening. Eventually, it will come out. The space is packed with dental wax, and the hide is sutured.

In an extremely parrot-mouthed horse, the first cheek tooth may have to be removed because the jaws are not set right. The upper tooth does not have a counterpart on the bottom to produce wear. As a result, when the horse closes his mouth, the top tooth will come into contact with the gum on the bottom jaw. This tooth-to-gum contact will occur on both sides of the mouth.

The same problem exists in the horse with an extremely undershot jaw, except that the upper gums will come into contact with the teeth on the lower jaw.

When the involved teeth are removed, the animal will show much improvement.

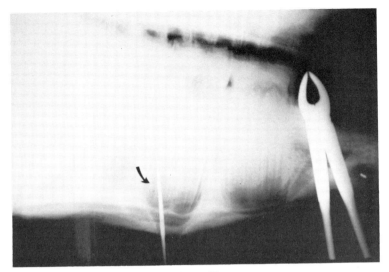

Figure 28

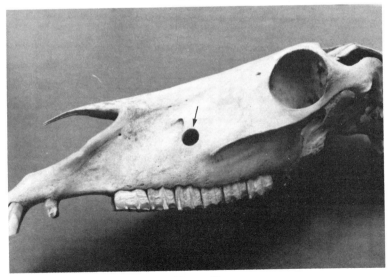

Figure 29

TOOTH ABNORMALITIES

Figure 30 shows an extreme example of a parrot-mouthed (overshot jaw) horse. Care must be taken with the first upper premolar, since there will be no opposite tooth on which it can wear. If this premolar grows too long it may interfere with chewing. In extreme cases, as in Figure 30, this premolar must be removed.

Figure 31 illustrates undershot. In this case, the lower first premolar may become too long because it does not have an opposite tooth on which to grind. Thus, it may have to be cut off or extracted in order for the animal to chew properly.

A piece of the baby corner incisor (*arrow*) is embedded in the gum of the 5-year-old horse shown in Figure 32. This piece of tooth should have been removed when the corner permanent tooth was emerging, thus preventing an abscess of the incisor.

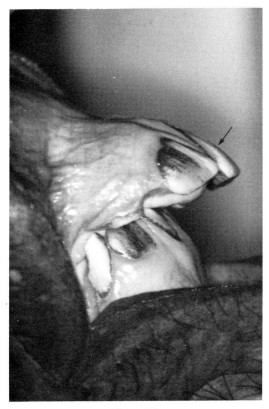

Figure 30

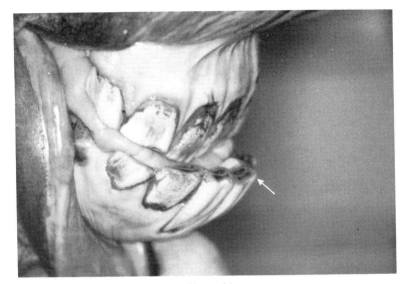

Figure 31

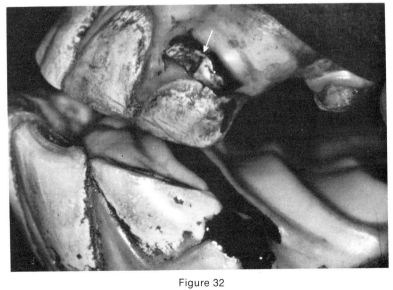

Figure 32

PARALYSIS OF THE TONGUE

A sure sign that a horse is suffering from paralysis of the tongue is that the animal will have an extreme thirst and will immerse his head in water up to his eyes. He is trying to drink but is unable to swallow. He has no fever. He will be salivating.

These signs are also a good indication of rabies, except that, in paralysis, the animal does not fear water. (A rabid animal also cannot drink but because of his fear of water would be incapable of immersing his head.)

If someone were to open the horse's mouth and grab his tongue, the horse would offer no resistance. An animal with paralysis of the tongue will slowly starve to death because of his inability to swallow.

An autopsy will reveal that both of the hyoid bones are fractured. The area surrounding the fracture will show evidence of decay and inflammation. In effect, the horse has lost the ability to bring his tongue back into a position for swallowing. To my knowledge there is no treatment for this condition.

PARALYSIS OF THE FALSE NOSTRILS, HIGH BLOWER

This condition is best diagnosed when the animal is ponied long and hard. Careful observation will show that each time the horse exhales, two enlargements about the size of an egg appear on the animal's face 2 inches behind the nostril. In addition, a loud fluttering sound, or roaring, can be heard.

The false nostril is a fold of skin that lies along the top of the inside of the true nostril and just under the face for a distance of about 3 or 4 inches. When this lining is removed by surgery, one can see that it resembles a finger from a person's glove.

To determine whether it is paralysis of the false nostrils or some problem in the larynx that is causing the animal to roar, two stitches should be applied through the flap of the false nostril up through the face. This will hold the lining to the skin. The animal should then be ponied. If the roaring stops, then paralysis of the false nostrils has been confirmed, and surgery can permanently correct the problem. The animal will completely recover in about three weeks and can be kept in light training during this time.

FACIAL PARALYSIS

Facial paralysis is sometimes seen in older horses as a result of a stroke or an injury to the skull. Whatever the cause, it affects the nerves that control the eyelid, lower lip, and the side of the head.

There is really no treatment for this problem.

SINUS INFECTIONS

Sinus infections usually involve the frontal sinuses below the eye. If the animal appears to have a headache (carries his head to one side) and has some swelling just below the eye and towards the middle of his head, then he probably has a sinus infection. If this area is tapped with the knuckles and sounds hollow, then the animal has no infection or only a slight infection. However, if it does not sound hollow, the sinuses are probably full of pus.

If the pus is in a liquid form, it can be irrigated through the nose. Figures 33 to 39 demonstrate the proper treatment of a milky discharge sinus infection from the nostrils.

Figure 33 shows a milky discharge from the nostrils *(arrow)*. This indicates that the pus has not solidified and is draining. The first step in treatment is to mix 10 ml of peroxide and 10 ml of tamed iodine.

Step two is to seal the end of a plastic cattle artificial inseminating tube. This is best done by burning the end of it. With an 18-gauge hypodermic needle, put several holes in the end of the tube along the sides. Using your thumb as a guide, pass the tube *(arrow)* back along the floor of the nasal passage (Fig. 34).

Fill a syringe *(arrow)* with the peroxide and iodine mixture

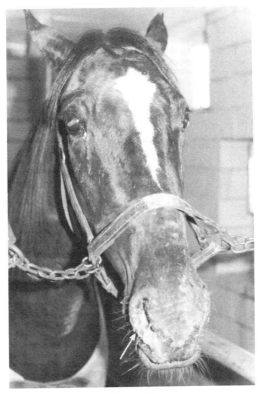

Figure 33

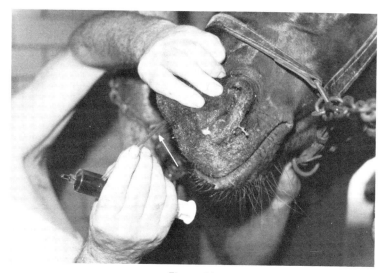

Figure 34

and attach it to the open end of the tube (Fig. 35). Spray the sinus area daily for 10 days.

If the tear (lacrimal) duct is involved, pass a *tom cat* catheter up the tear duct in the nose and flush with 10 ml of a mild salt solution (saline) daily until the duct has cleared (Figs. 36 and 37).

In complicated cases pass oxygen through a mixture of steroid and antibiotic (Fig. 38). Usually, an ounce of predniso-lone and an ounce of neomycin are mixed with 2 ounces of water. In order to administer the oxygen, a mask can be made from a small plastic pail and an old halter. The oxygen comes in through the bottom of the pail (Fig. 39). Treat the animal twice daily (for 20 minutes) for about 10 days, or until the infection has cleared.

If the pus has hardened, then it must be tapped through the face. A *trephine,* or round saw, is used to bore a $\frac{1}{2}$-inch hole through the skull. A wick soaked in equal parts of iodine and mineral oil is worked into the sinus. The animal is then stitched, leaving part of the wick exposed so that it can be pulled out a little bit each day. This procedure keeps the hole open and allows the sinus to drain.

A sinus infection usually starts as a viral infection that is complicated by a bacterial infection. It is the bacterial infection that causes the pus to form. The difficulty in treating a bacterial infection in the sinus is that penicillin levels cannot be raised enough in the sinus to kill the bacteria. Therefore, irrigation is necessary.

Occasionally, a sinus infection is the result of a split tooth. In this case, the sinus must be tapped and the fractured tooth driven out, thereby allowing proper drainage from the infected sinus. Healing occurs naturally.

In all throat, nose, and sinus infections of the horse, large doses of vitamin C (2000 mg daily) will aid recovery.

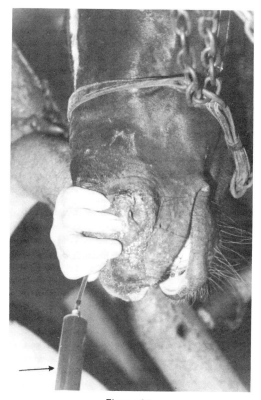

Figure 35

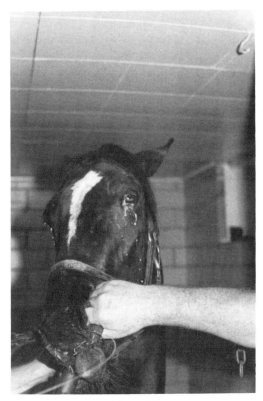

Figure 36

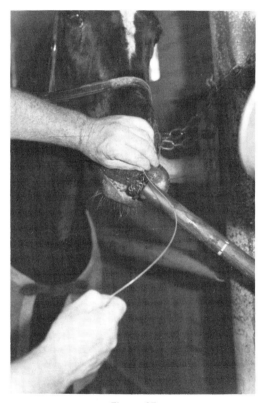

Figure 37

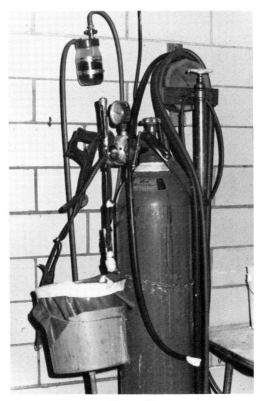

Figure 38

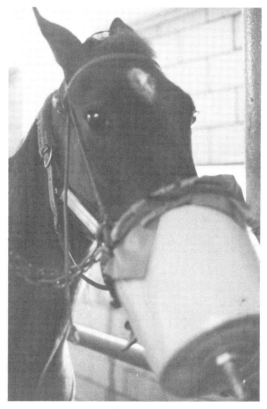

Figure 39

GUTTURAL POUCH INFECTION

The guttural pouches are saclike formations in the eustachian tube, which runs from the ear to the throat. These sacs, or cavities, can hold as much as a pint of fluid when full. In the race horse, these pouches may be the site of some hemorrhage during a race. They are full of blood vessels, and any infection, especially a fungal infection, tends to deprive the veins and arteries of their supportive tissue.

The horse is the only domestic animal with a guttural pouch. When infected, the guttural pouch will sometimes distend for as much as 6 inches down the *jugular furl* (Fig. 40).

Nosebleeds during exercise or when under stress indicate that the horse may have a guttural pouch infection. However, not all nosebleeds are from the guttural pouches.

In the past, guttural pouch infections were treated by establishing drainage at the back of the jaw. Today, a plastic catheter (tube) can be inserted through the pharyngeal opening of the guttural pouch. The other end of the catheter is sutured to the inside of the nose. The catheter facilitates drainage and allows the pouch to be irrigated daily with suitable antibiotics. Nitrofurazone (Furacin, by Eaton) and acriflavine are two drugs of choice. Generally, 30 ml of a 0.2 per cent solution of nitrofurazone would be sufficient. Irrigation is done by attaching a

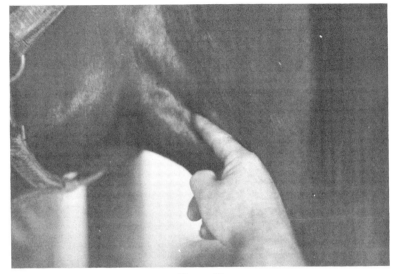

Figure 40

syringe to the end of the catheter and forcing the drug into the guttural pouch region.

The degree of infection can be determined by passing an endoscope (an instrument that allows the veterinarian to inspect the throat) with a curved tip through the pharyngeal opening into the pouch. In this manner, the walls of the pouch can be examined visibly. A low-grade infection may not produce bleeding but will result in a nasal discharge, especially when the animal lowers his head; the fluid, usually clear and viscous and without odor, simply drains out of the pouches and runs out the nose.

Guttural pouch infections generally follow equine influenza, strangles, or any viral infection affecting the throat.

MIDDLE EAR INFECTION

If the horse circles in one direction or loses his balance on either his right or his left side, he is probably suffering from a middle ear infection, since the middle ear is primarily responsible for the animal maintaining his balance.

Unlike the wobbler, who loses coordination to both the left and right sides, the horse with a middle ear infection will lose his balance only when he is turned either to the right or to the left.

Middle ear infections may be due to guttural pouch infections. As the first step in treatment, a sample is taken from the guttural pouch with a swab and cultured. An antibiotic is then chosen that will most effectively kill the bacteria causing the infection. Lasix (Hoescht-Roussel) is the drug of choice. Water balance in the body is also important, and a diuretic may be necessary.

SOFT PALATE

It is not known whether a horse is born with or later develops an abnormal soft palate. An abnormal soft palate interferes with the passage of air into the larynx. (Figure 41 shows a soft palate [arrow] being held by forceps.) When the free end of the soft palate is drawn back over the epiglottis, the horse has difficulty in breathing and emits a noise somewhat like a gurgle or snore. This noise increases if the animal tries to breathe through his mouth while galloping. The noise made by a horse with a soft palate is much louder than that made by a roarer or an animal with a collapsed nostril condition. This feature helps to distinguish the three conditions.

Treatment is to remove surgically the free end of the palate. The horse is put on his back on an operating table. An anesthetic tube is inserted and then removed from the horse's throat, and a light is put in the animal's mouth to illuminate the soft palate. The larynx is entered, and the surgeon grasps the end of the palate with long forceps and surgically removes the affected end. As soon as hemorrhage is controlled, the anesthetic tube is reinserted, and the incision is sutured.

Recovery requires about three weeks. There may be one side effect: If too much of the palate has been cut away, some water will run out of the horse's nose when he drinks quickly.

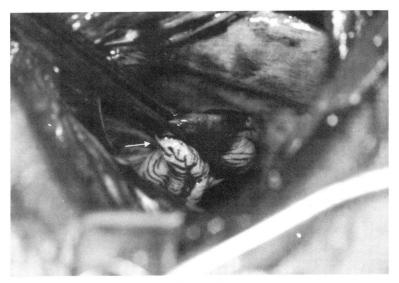

Figure 41

ROARER (PARALYSIS OF THE MUSCLES TO THE ARYTENOID CARTILAGES)

Two ventricles, one on each side of the voice box (larynx), lie just inside the windpipe (trachea) and are bordered by the vocal cords. They resemble a fish gill and are about ½ inch long (Fig. 42). In a normal horse, these ventricles pull back to the side of the larynx when the horse inhales. However, when the muscles to the arytenoids are paralyzed, the ventricle does not pull back to the side of the larynx, causing an obstruction in the air passage, which in turn produces a roaring sound when the animal is running.

In most cases only the left ventricle is involved, but occasionally the right or both ventricles are affected.

It is thought that roaring is due to infections in the surrounding area or to infections that somehow affect the nerves to the surrounding tissue. Figure 43 shows herpes virus lesions, appearing as water bubbles on the left ventricle (*arrows*), which no doubt were the cause of the paralysis of the left arytenoid cartilage in this case. (The instrument is inserted into the ventricle to remove the lining.) Perhaps distemper involving the lymph glands to that area or a fungal infection in the guttural pouches near the base of the ear is responsible. In any event,

50

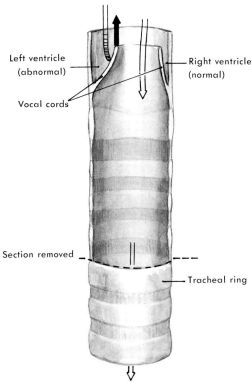

Figure 42

an endoscope can be used to determine whether a horse has this condition.

Treatment consists of removing the lining of the ventricle by surgery and then suturing the mouth of the ventricle closed, thereby giving the horse a larger hole through which to breathe.

Large-headed, long-necked horses tend to develop into roarers more readily than small-headed, short-necked horses.

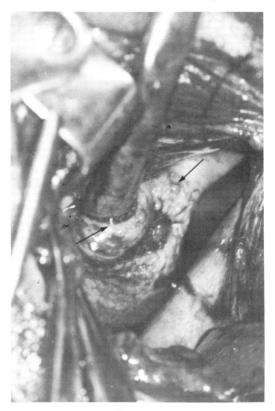

Figure 43

This tendency is due to the fact that the recurrent nerve to the left side of the larynx, which loops around the aorta, is thought to be too short on long-necked horses, and as a result it becomes paralyzed owing to the animal turning his head away from the nerve at a sharp angle.

THE CHOKING HORSE

A choking horse will choke down without making any noise. The horse may even fall down from lack of air. If the affected animal is a race horse, the jockey may say something to the effect that "I couldn't keep him in the hole behind the other horse because he was choking off."

The windpipe is a flexible hose, much like the hose in a car radiator. It is made up of many rings, each of which is held together by a small membrane (Fig. 44). The first ring is attached to the larynx (voice box or "Adam's apple") by a thin, membranous ligament. When this ligament loses its elasticity, it bulges into the air passage each time the horse breathes.

When a rider draws hard on the reins, the horse's nose is pulled toward the animal's chest, producing a sharp angle between the jaw bone and the neck. In the choking horse, the windpipe, because of the loose ligament, folds up behind the larynx and shuts off all, or nearly all, of the air. Without air the animal will stagger slightly or may fall if he is not pulled up.

This condition can be treated surgically. The operation consists of dissecting away the fatty tissue between the larynx and the first ring of the windpipe. Two wire sutures are then placed through these two parts, drawing them tightly together.

In a few weeks the windpipe heals tightly to the larynx and the choking no longer occurs.

This operation is sometimes performed at the same time as a roaring operation in the ventricle of the larynx.

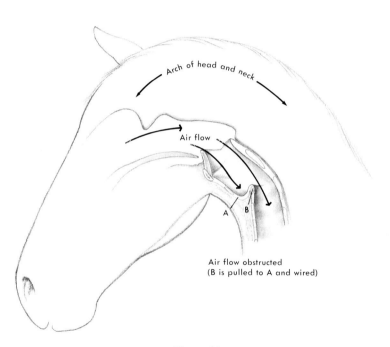

Arch of head and neck

Air flow

A   B

Air flow obstructed
(B is pulled to A and wired)

Figure 44

PHARYNGITIS (SORE THROAT)

Pharyngitis is an acute or chronic inflammation of the pharynx (throat) that results in a persistent cough. This condition is thought to be initiated by a virus followed by a secondary bacterial infection. The bacteria grow in colonies and form a mucus-like coating over the inside of the throat, making the infection difficult to treat. The infection can be seen with a laryngoscope: Minute droplets tend to hang from the walls and ceiling of the pharynx, and sometimes the epiglottis is involved and will appear to have small water blisters on it.

The best treatment is for the animal to inhale oxygen filled with steroid and cortisone. (See pages 43 and 44.)

Supportive treatment is necessary. I generally give the horse large daily doses of vitamin C, iodine, and an antibiotic such as penicillin-streptomycin. Iodine that is fed to horses is called *ethylenediamine dihydriodide*. In severe cases I use 10 ml of 1 per cent solution of Lugal's iodine and spray it directly over the tongue once a day for 10 days.

The acute symptoms will disappear; however, the animal is sometimes left with a chronic pharyngitis and will require periodic treatment throughout his racing or work career.

NOSEBLEEDING

Nosebleeding may originate from the sinuses, guttural pouch, or lungs. To determine the exact site of the bleeding, an endoscope is inserted in the nostril. If a varicose vein can be seen in the sinus or at the pharyngeal opening of the guttural pouch, this area can be considered the source of the bleeding. An endoscope with a curved tip can be inserted directly into the guttural pouch, and thus it can be determined if the bleeding is coming from this area.

Bleeding from the lungs constitutes a serious problem. If a horse is hemorrhaging from the nose after a race or work, a needle should be inserted between two rings of the trachea. If blood-tinged froth is drawn out by the needle, then the bleeding problem originates in the lungs, not in the guttural pouch or the sinuses.

Most bleeding can be controlled, irrespective of its origin. A few hours before a horse is to race or work, he should be given 3 ml of Lasix (Hoescht-Roussel). Lasix drops the blood pressure and relieves the edema in the lung, giving the animal more breathing capacity and lessening the stress on the lung tissue.

Vitamin K, administered either by hypodermic needle or by mixing with feed, tends to increase the quality of the blood clotting, thereby preventing hemorrhage. Conjugated estrogens (female hormones) also encourage clotting.

If the bleeding originates in the sinuses or guttural pouch, and the vein is accessible, the vein can be cauterized by the use of cold cauterization.

RESPIRATORY DISEASES

HEAVES (BROKEN WIND, PULMONARY EMPHYSEMA)

Heaves is characterized by a dry, hacking cough. When coughing, the horse usually lowers his head, and the nostrils and the rectum are generally dilated (stretched wide open). The heave line, the line along the border of the last rib near the flank, will jerk just after the animal exhales normally. This jerking or heaving motion is due to the effort by the body to rid itself of the air that is trapped in the lungs.

Air becomes trapped in saccules that are formed when the walls of the air sacs in the lungs break down. Instead of having multiple, tiny air sacs in his lungs, a horse with heaves has large sacs that are formed by the breakdown of these walls. These new sacs can vary in size and may be microscopic or as large as a fist. Air gets trapped in these large saccules, and the animal cannot exhale properly.

Any horse with this problem should have his hay and grain soaked with water to prevent inhalation of dust. Oral antihistamines can be given to the animal on a daily basis. Iodine supplements will help dry the discharge in the lungs. Ethylenediamine dihydriodide in a palatable base works well. Forty grains (2 tablespoons) is usually sufficient. Follow the directions on the bottle.

In the past, belladonna leaves or large doses of an arsenic preparation were used to relieve the symptoms of heaves. However, these treatments were only effective for about a day. Neither was a cure. Acupuncture is reported to be effective in relieving this condition.

Dimethyl sulfoxide (DMSO) has been used experimentally to cure heaves with very encouraging results. The dosage is 2.5 ml mixed with 20 ml of 100 mg per ml of chloramphenicol.

Recently a new drug used chiefly in the treatment of lung worms in calves has been tried with some success. The drug is called dictyzide. (This drug may be difficult to obtain.) Ten ml is injected in both sides of the neck; two days later the dose is repeated. Dictyzide exerts action on the bronchial muscles, thereby increasing the breathing capacity of the animal.

The preceding discussion describes severe heaves. However, some horses develop this condition in a mild form that is difficult to differentiate from a straight viral cough. A horse with a viral cough will most likely demonstrate a rise in temperature.

BRONCHIAL PNEUMONIA

The symptoms of bronchial pneumonia include the following: a temperature of 104° to 106° F (normal is 100° F), difficulty in breathing, nasal discharge, depression, dull eyes, coughing, and a rasping, cracking sound in the horse's rib cage.

Although a virus is a causative agent of many pneumonias, a bacterial organism is usually responsible for bronchial pneumonia.

There are many drugs that will cure bronchial pneumonia. Any good sulfa drug or antibiotic will handle the situation well.* The animal should be kept in a well-ventilated, warm, dry stall.

---

*Because sulfa drugs can cause kidney damage, they should be used only under qualified supervision. If a penicillin-streptomycin combination is used, an insufficient amount will endanger the horse's life more than will an overdose. Therefore, I suggest that an adult horse should be given 20 ml daily of most commercial brands until the animal has recovered.

Since electrolyte and fluid balance in the horse's body is very important in controlling temperature, all decisions in this regard should be made by your veterinarian.

COMMON COLD

The common cold in the horse is harder to treat than pneumonia. In fact, there is an old saying that states: "If you treat a cold it takes three weeks to cure, and if you don't treat it, it takes 21 days."

If the animal is not eating, he should be given intravenous electrolytes and amino acids and supported with vitamin supplements. If the horse has a throat infection in addition to his cold, the procedure for treating pharyngitis should be used (see pages 43 and 44).

The horse should be kept warm and out of drafts. He should not work and should not exercise and should be given high levels of vitamin C and a suitable iodine supplement.

Forty grains (2 tablespoons) of ethylenediamine dihydriodide is the usual dosage for most commercial preparations. Follow the directions on the bottle.

If the animal has a high fever, injections of an antibiotic should be administered for four or five days.

DISTEMPER (STRANGLES)

Symptoms of distemper are (1) the horse holds his head low, (2) he has a discharge from his nose, (3) his jaw generally takes on a rounded appearance due to swollen glands, (4) he is generally depressed, (5) he has difficulty in swallowing, and (6) his temperature ranges between 104° and 106°F (normal is 100°F).

Distemper is caused by the bacterium *Streptococcus equi* and is a contagious condition. The bacterium is transmitted from one horse to another in saliva, nasal discharges, and the discharge from the abscesses under the jaw. Horses that eat or drink from the same buckets or feeders are susceptible.

Outbreaks of distemper usually occur after a horse show or race meet, and the animals without immunity will inevitably contract the disease. Foals and yearlings are generally affected more severely than older horses. However, since there is no lasting immunity, an older horse may also be susceptible.

Breeding farms are quite concerned about this disease because of the possibility that mares brought in from other farms or localities for breeding may have the disease. Young foals are very susceptible to this condition.

Distemper seems to occur in cycles. Outbreaks appear about every 10 years. Once an animal contracts the disease, he then has a degree of immunity that may last for a short time or for many years.

If distemper is not treated, complications such as pneumonia can kill the animal. However, many animals will recover on their own. The elevated temperature will remain until the glands under the jaw rupture. Once they rupture, allowing pus to exude from the wounds, the temperature will drop.

Complicated strangles, sometimes known as *bastard strangles,* occurs when the infection develops in the lymph nodes and other parts of the body. When the infection is in the intestines, the animal has a low-grade colic and pus is visible in the stool. When infection occurs in the lymph glands of the lungs, the horse develops a low-grade pneumonia. I have even had horses develop abscesses in the chest and along the hocks. All the horses that I have seen with complicated strangles have died.

Treatment consists of basic good care. The barn should be well ventilated and kept clean. It also is helpful to spray the walls with a disinfectant. The animal's temperature should be controlled by giving adequate doses of penicillin-streptomycin (20 ml daily, as required), and the infected glands should be encouraged to rupture. A mild liniment rubbed over the area will encourage this. Once drainage begins, the wound should be syringed with peroxide and a diluted solution of iodine.

If, when the gland ruptures, the hole is not large enough to permit good drainage, a small incision should be made to improve the flow. The incision may leave a scar, but it will eventually disappear.

It is almost impossible to prevent distemper. When feasible, affected animals should be kept isolated from other horses, and separate buckets and utensils should be used.

Vaccines now available are not adequate, and some have even made the animals sicker than if they had contracted the disease. I hope that a good vaccine will be developed in the near future.

PARASITIC INFESTATIONS

In addition to good feed, control of parasites is probably *the* most important consideration in keeping a horse healthy.

STRONGYLES (BLOOD WORMS)

Strongyles, principally *Strongylus vulgaris* and *Strongylus edidymis,* the two large species of blood worms, live on the lining of the large intestine, where they lay their eggs. At this stage of infestation, the only problem the organisms create is that they tend to live on the blood in the gut wall and reduce the total hemoglobin of the blood.

Once the egg leaves the body through the manure, it hatches into the first stage larva. Before it becomes infectious, the larva goes through three stages, shedding its skin at each stage. When it reaches the third stage, it is infective. It lives in box stalls and paddocks and may survive for months in the right environment.

When a horse swallows a third stage larva, it passes into the stomach, then to the colon and cecum. At this point it enters the lining of the intestines, sheds its skin once again, and becomes a fourth stage larva. This fourth stage larva has the ability to leave the intestinal wall and enter the small arterial and artery walls.

The larvae migrate for about 50 to 60 days, and some actually find their way into the anterior mesenteric artery. The body builds fibrin around many of these larvae, and they become trapped here. However, this is not their normal route.

Normally, after 50 or 60 days, the migrating larvae break out of the arterial walls into the blood stream and travel until they reach the outside lining of the gut. Here they cause a small nodule to form. (The nodule is noticeable on postmortem examination.)

Sometime later (it usually takes about six months for the cycle to complete itself), the larvae enter the lumen of the gut and become adults. These adults are able to lay eggs, thus completing the life cycle.

However, a few larvae are not able to complete the cycle because they have become trapped in the mesenteric artery, where large bundles of fibrin build up. This build-up partially occludes the artery, which causes poor circulation to the gut, resulting in colic and several other indigestion-like symptoms.

Some of these larvae enter the aorta. However, they will never complete their life cycle because they cannot penetrate the heavy elastic layer in the wall of the large blood vessels.

There is some controversy as to whether the larvae are able to reach the iliac arteries. I find that if there is reduced circulation to the back legs of the horse, rectal palpation will reveal thrombosis in these arteries, similar to that found in the mesentery. Therefore, I feel that the thrombosis is caused by blood worms, although I have never seen live larvae in the thrombi.

This thickening is reversible. This can be carried out by worming with 160 gm of Thibenzole (Merck, Sharp, Dohme) followed in 10 days by a second worming with 80 gm of Thibenzole. The thickened iliac arteries can be palpated by a rectal examination and repalpated following the second worming. This method of treatment is very effective and kills the parasites without hurting the horse.

I cannot stress enough the importance of the control of this parasite. Dirty box stalls and overpopulated paddocks will certainly encourage the spread of blood worm infestation. As a control measure, the horse should be wormed, preferably tubed, at least four times a year with a medicine formulated to destroy blood worms. There is a simple test for the presence of mature blood worms that most veterinary laboratories can perform, provided they have a sample of the animal's stool.

Fecal samples should be collected at various times over a 24-hour period. Strongyle eggs may not always be present if only one sample is taken. Recently, I found an animal which had 12 to 15 eggs per field; this same horse had been tested a few days earlier by another veterinarian who had determined that the animal was relatively free of blood worms.

As of this writing there is no definite test for larvae in the blood stream.

Although phenolthiazine is a very effective drug to use in tubing, too large a dose will produce anemia and therefore will defeat the purpose of worming. Most of the piperazines are effective against the small blood worm. For large strongyles, I prefer tubing with a carbon disulfide–piperazine combination. (Parvex, by Upjohn. Follow recommended dosage.) Thibenzole is also effective.

Anemia is one symptom of blood worm infestation. If a laboratory or veterinarian is not available to determine the blood count or the hemoglobin level, then roll back the animal's lip and look at the gum line. If it appears to be pale, go to another horse, an animal you think is normal, and compare the color of his gum line. The gum line of the normal horse should be much darker in color.

In most cases of blood worm infestation, the hair coat will be rough. In the spring the animal fails to shed properly. However, I have seen well groomed, apparently healthy horses with heavy infestations.

Chronic colic following a meal is sometimes caused by a large number of blood worm larvae in the mesenteric artery. Occasionally, after running a hard quarter mile, a horse will kick at the ground, stamp his feet, and in severe cases want to lie down. In less severe cases the horse will simply show a lameness that will leave shortly after he has come to rest. This kind of behavior can mean that there is a thickening in the iliac artery that prevents blood from flowing down the leg. A rectal examination by a veterinarian to determine the character of the pulse on the iliac artery will indicate whether there has been blood worm damage to the arteries leading to the back legs.

Another test for determining the presence of blood worms in these arteries involves the two large veins that run down the inside of the back legs. These veins are always flat when the horse is in flight. If the animal is stopped quickly, these veins normally take on a rounded appearance or fill up after five seconds or, at the most, eight seconds. If it takes longer than eight seconds, there was not enough blood flowing down the leg while the animal was in flight. On examination, the back legs will be several degrees colder than the front legs.

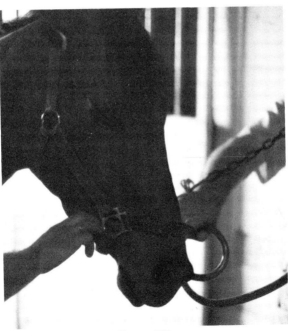

Figure 44A

ASCARIDES (STOMACH WORMS, ROUND WORMS)

All species of animals have ascarides, including man. These parasites are not a major problem in the adult-aged horse because he seems to develop an immunity to them. However, ascarides are a problem in the young foal, who can die of colic because the worms form a ball in the bowel. This may happen after the foal is 42 days old or sometimes even younger.

If you suspect that a foal has a large number of stomach worms, give him 1 tablespoon of piperazine; this dose will kill most of the worms. Follow this with a tubing (described on page 70). A foal should be wormed at the ages of 42 days, 6 months, 8 months, and 12 months.

Most medicines formulated to kill blood worms will also kill stomach worms; however, I believe piperazine is the drug of choice for the round worm.

It is thought that some of the larvae of the ascarid gather in the throat area; therefore, they may cause coughing in some horses, particularly in young foals. I have found that worming will stop coughing in these horses. The foal may begin coughing as early as four weeks if he does indeed have ascarides.

The ascarid lays its eggs in the intestine. They, in turn,

travel through the blood stream to the liver. From the liver they migrate through the blood to the lungs, invade the air sacs, and then move up into the windpipe. Eventually, they enter the gullet and are swallowed. Once in the stomach they become adult worms. The eggs that are passed to the outside through the manure (Fig. 45) *embryonate* (partially hatch) and may remain dormant for many months until they are swallowed by a grazing horse.

I believe that a pregnant mare with ascarides passes them on to her foal. The theory is that the eggs do not know the difference between the liver of the mare and the liver of the foal; therefore, they become established in the liver of the foal before it is born. They complete the life cycle after the foal takes its first breath.

Figure 45

BOTFLIES

A large number of bots (larvae of botflies) in the stomach of the horse can cause death.

There are several kinds of botflies, and they are known by where they lay their eggs on the horse. Some lay their eggs on the animal's chin, while others deposit them around the nose or on the legs and shoulders. These eggs are small, yellow particles that are quite noticeable on the hair. The adult botfly generally lays these eggs in the late summer and early fall.

When the animal scratches himself with his teeth or licks himself with his tongue, some of the eggs enter his mouth. From there, they eventually work their way into the stomach.

In temperate climates, the bot starts to develop about the middle of January. In southern Canada, most bots do not appear until March. However, I have seen bots as late as the middle of June in horses that have not been treated. The larvae can be seen in the manure, are reddish in color, and are about one quarter of an inch wide and about three quarters of an inch long.

The bot is best controlled while it is still on the animal's coat. When a cloth soaked with coal oil is rubbed on the area where the eggs are clustered, most of them will be destroyed. The coal oil removes the grease from the eggs and they dehydrate (dry out). A serrated table knife or a safety razor can then be used to scrape the eggs off the coat.

Once the bots enter the body, however, you must wait until spring to remove them.

The common medicines used to kill blood worms and ascarides do not kill bots. Carbon disulfide, however, has proved effective. In the past, carbon disulfide was given by capsule. Now it can be obtained in powder form mixed with piperazine. When these drugs are dissolved in water and administered to the horse by way of a stomach tube, they will kill bots, ascarides, and blood worms.

I believe that if a horse is wormed for bots about the first of March and a few are found, he should be wormed again at the end of April so that it can be positively determined that the animal has no more bots.

PINWORMS

A pinworm is a short, white worm with a thin tail that inhabits the rectum of the horse.

The most common sign of a pinworm infestation is that the animal will rub his rear against a fence post or the side of his stall. If you notice that the animal has no hair at the root of the tail then you should suspect a pinworm infestation. However, check the skin to be sure that he does not have mange.

I believe that any worm medicine that kills blood worms will kill pinworms. Piperazine is quite effective.

LICE

Another parasite that causes discomfort and poor health in the horse is the louse. Lice can be seen chiefly in the mane and around the tailhead. The hair will be oily, and there will be a great deal of dandruff. If a hot lamp is held next to the animal, the insects will crawl to the surface of the hair.

If the animal has a long coat, he should be clipped and treated with any recommended louse powder. One or two applications should be sufficient.

In addition, the stalls should be sprayed with creosol.

DERMATOLOGIC
DISORDERS

DANDRUFF

Dandruff, especially along the mane, is often associated with lice but it can also be a symptom of malnutrition. If the horse has dandruff but his coat is not oily, the animal is probably not getting a proper diet.

Sometimes a slight skin infection may be present, and a good iodine shampoo will clear it up. A selenium shampoo may also be effective.

HORSE POX

Horse pox is a fungal infection that may affect part or all of the body. It is a small pimply condition that oozes a serum-like pus (see Fig. 46). The pus forms a scab, and the infection will spread to other parts of the body.

The best treatment is to apply a good fungicide and, in my opinion, the best fungicide is tamed iodine soap. Bathe the animal, brush all the scabs off with a soft brush, and let the soap dry on his body.

Potassium iodide should be added to the animal's feed. For a 1000 pound animal, administer 1 tablespoon of potassium iodide crystals daily for about 10 days or until symptoms of iodine poisoning develop.

The principal symptom of iodine poisoning is excessive tearing.

The cured lesion will be gray, and the hair around it will fall out. In time most of the hair will grow back; however, it may be a slightly different shade. The animal will carry these marks for the rest of his life.

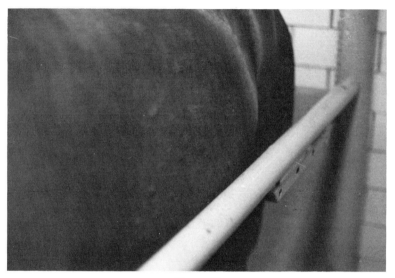

Figure 46

COMMON GIRTH DISEASE

Common girth disease is a rash in which small pimples exude a serum-like substance that forms a small scab. This condition usually occurs in areas where the saddle or harness touches the animal or it may appear over the entire body.

It is a fungal infection and it is spread from one horse to another on curry combs, brushes, saddles, and harnesses.

Almost any good fungicide such as tamed iodine soap will handle the disease. Sometimes secondary infections will set in, and antibiotic salves will be required to treat the larger lesions.

VIRAL WARTS

Viral warts appear suddenly around the nose or ears of the horse. They are not very contagious, although more than one horse in a herd will usually be infected. In fact, they are more unsightly than dangerous.

This condition should be treated by rubbing or painting castor oil over the affected area. Occasionally, if some of the bigger warts are broken off, the horse will become self-vaccinated and the warts will vanish almost as quickly as they appeared.

MANGE

Mange, a skin disorder caused by mange mites, on a horse is quite rare, but when it does occur it usually affects the tailhead.

The first symptom is the loss of hair at the tailhead; this is due to the animal rubbing his tail against a fence post or the side of his stall. This rubbing can result in deeper wounds that exude blood and serum from a secondary infection. However, pinworms will also cause him to behave in this manner.

Diagnosis is made by examining a small skin scraping under a microscope in order to identify the mange mite. A fecal test will determine whether the problem is caused by pinworms.

RINGWORM

Ringworm is a fungal infection that affects the skin of the horse and is characterized by a round discoloration that is about the size of a quarter. Unlike horse pox, these lesions are gray, dry, and scaly and usually cover most of the body (Fig. 47).

In most cases iodine preparations are sufficient treatment. The affected areas should be washed with iodine soap, and a salve should be applied. A simple formula for salve is iodine, sulfur, and lard. Rub this mixture onto the affected area. Be sure to use gloves or to disinfect your hands immediately afterward.

Be careful not to use contaminated brushes or combs on other animals because the infection may be spread in this manner.

Figure 47

SPOROTRICHOSIS

This problem is caused by a fungus, *Sporothrix schenckii*. This fungus gains entrance to the skin through scratches or wounds and will produce swellings that are about the size of a pea. These organisms can also spread through the lymph duct system and produce a linear swelling.

Sometimes the swellings will become soft, come to a head, and break, releasing pus. If they do not break then they will remain in a dormant stage for a long period.

Figure 48 shows a hard lesion in the stifle area. Unlike calcium that forms at the head of the fibula, this lesion moves with the skin. Treatment consists of passing a cotton wick soaked in equal parts of mineral oil and iodine through the lesion (Fig. 49).

When treating this condition, keep the affected areas clean by washing them with tamed iodine soap. Scrub the swellings until the heads come off; this will allow the pus to drain. Sodium iodide given intravenously or potassium iodide mixed in the feed, along with thorough cleansing of the affected areas, should clear up the condition.

Caution: Prolonged use of potassium iodide produces iodine poisoning. (The symptoms are described on page 80.)

Sporotrichosis can be contagious but it can be transmitted only through an open wound.

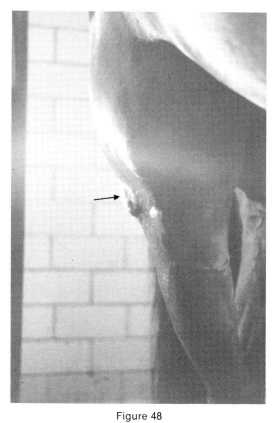

Figure 48

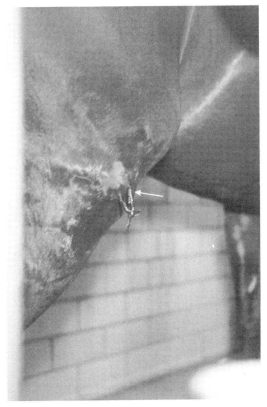

Figure 49

ALSAC CLOVER POISONING

This white clover, if not properly cured in the field, may sometimes produce a hivelike condition on the white part of the horse's nose.

To treat, simply remove the cause, the alsac clover.

BEE STINGS

The histamine action on the tissue as a result of a bee sting can produce massive edema or swelling where the animal was stung. Since the horse is usually stung on the head, the lips and tongue are the areas that will swell.

A bee sting is best treated by injecting the animal with an antihistamine (follow label directions for proper dosage) and bathing the swollen area with a light astringent such as zinc lotion or cold tea. Epinephrine (adrenaline) is also effective.

DIARRHEA

A foal will develop a slight case of diarrhea at nine days of age because it is at this time that the mare experiences "foal heat." A change in the mother's feed can also cause the foal to develop diarrhea. This can easily be controlled by feeding the foal some kalin and pectin, possibly combined with some sulfa. In addition, there are many other preparations readily available at any drugstore or from the veterinarian. Adequate dosages are usually given on the bottle.

Acute diarrhea in the adult horse may be due to *colitis X,* a disease that is not fully understood. The disease causes a profuse watery discharge from the anus; the animal can actually pass gallons of fluid in this way. The mucous membranes turn purple, and the temperature drops below normal. Unless massive fluid therapy is carried out immediately, death is almost certain.

I normally provide intravenous replacement through a 14-gauge needle in both jugular veins at the same time. Sometimes 10 to 20 gallons of fluid must be replaced before the diarrhea can be checked.

There are two drugs available that will stop the motion of the bowel, thereby reducing the excessive diarrhea: Viraform (CIBA) and Biosol M (Upjohn). Both of these drugs, when used as prescribed, will check fairly severe diarrhea.

Causes of diarrhea can vary from the ingestion of moldy hay to extreme nervousness. In the case of a nervous horse, a good policy is to feed him a handful of brewers' yeast daily.

In some horses prolonged diarrhea will cause a loss of intestinal bacteria, which are a normal part of the digestive process. When this happens, the bacteria have to be replenished. This can be done by taking a shovelful of manure from a healthy horse (one who is free of worms), soaking it in a pail of water overnight, straining off the solids, and then pumping the fluid into the horse's stomach. Some drug companies sell prepared cultures for replenishing the bacteria.

URINARY
SYSTEM
DISORDERS

One of the most common complaints that a horse owner makes to a veterinarian is, "Doc, he can't make his water." This could be due to a bladder condition or to muscle tie-up. The urine collects in the bladder and the animal can get no relief until suitable drugs are given to make him urinate.

Infections of the bladder may be primary or occasionally may occur in a mare after she foals. The mare may get cervicitis or vaginitis, and the infection will make its way directly to the bladder. The infection may not remain there; it can eventually produce a kidney infection. The most common symptom of infection in the mare is that she passes small amounts of urine quite frequently.

The proper treatment of a routine bladder infection can be determined from the results of a bacterial culture of the urine. With this information a proper antibiotic can be selected with which to treat the animal.

In areas where hard water is used, the bladder may simply be irritated, not infected. Stones form and plug the neck of the bladder. Because the animal cannot urinate, he becomes depressed and his stomach becomes swollen. When a gelding or stallion has stones that plug the neck of the bladder, a small incision is made in the penis where it crosses the pelvis. The lining of the penis (urethra) is rolled out and spread with forceps. Special forceps can be passed through this opening into the bladder. With one arm in the rectum, the veterinarian can palpate the bladder and move the stone to the forceps. The stone can then be drawn out. If the stone is very large, it can be broken and removed in pieces.

After the stone or stones have been removed, the incision is kept open for a few days until the horse once again begins to pass urine properly. The urethra is then sewed and the animal will urinate normally.

Treatment for a mare is much simpler because the urethra, which lies on the floor of the vagina, is very accessible, and the stone can be easily removed.

Occasionally, for some unknown reason, a horse will have a spasm at the neck of the bladder. This situation can be relieved by tranquilizing the animal and then administering 3 ml of Lasix (Hoescht-Roussel). Lasix causes the neck of the bladder to relax, and the horse will be able to urinate.

KIDNEY INFECTION

One characteristic of a horse with a kidney infection is that the animal will have a sore back. If you press your fingers down hard along the backbone at a point about a foot ahead of the pelvis, the animal will show great pain. He may also stand with a hunched back.

Frequently, the horse's hair has a peculiar odor that is very suggestive of urine. The urine in the stall has an extremely strong ammonia odor and is very heavy or viscous. The animal has a tendency to urinate often.

If it is determined that the horse is suffering from a kidney infection, the kidneys should be flushed with 3 ml of Lasix (Hoescht-Roussel). It is also beneficial to run a bottle of electrolytes into the jugular vein. This, too, will help flush the kidneys. If this treatment does not prove successful, a culture of the urine will determine the type of infection; the appropriate antibiotic can then be used to eliminate the causative organisms.

Kidney infections in foals usually result from joint ill, a condition that is almost always fatal. Some foals may recover from the symptoms of joint ill (swollen joints and inflamed navel cord); however, they will not thrive. I have performed post mortems on horses that acquired joint ill at birth and lived to be 2 years old; I found that they had only one functioning kidney. The other kidney would be best described as a "sac of pus."

Sometimes the kidney was functioning at half its capacity. Harmful bacteria apparently localize in the kidney and cause this kind of destruction.

Proper care of the kidneys in working horses is extremely important. Mild diuretics (drugs that help increase the volume of urine, thereby flushing the kidneys) should be administered to the animal after a race or heavy work. However, excessive use of diuretics is harmful and produces dehydration and bladder irritation.

When a horse is worked hard, the kidney must work even harder to filter out impurities. Therefore, I do not feel that it does any harm to help the system out a little as long as it is done in moderation.

NERVOUS
HABITS

CRIBBING

The horse is a great habit-forming individual, and probably one of his most common nervous habits is cribbing. The cribbing horse grabs the edge of a door, water pail, or feed tub, ducks his chin back, and sucks air into his stomach. This habit may become a health problem because the animal may begin to substitute air for food.

If you suspect this problem, look at the horse's front teeth. If they are worn on the outside edge, then the horse is a cribber. I believe that one reason why a horse becomes a cribber is that his teeth were not properly looked after when he began to shed the first incisors as a 2-year-old. At that age, nature tells him that if he bites on something, it will help loosen the 2-year-old caps. The biting then becomes a habit. Figure 50, *A* and *B*, shows a severe cribber. The table surfaces of the incisors of this horse are worn to the point where the animal has difficulty biting grass.

It is almost impossible to stop a horse from cribbing. An operation can be performed that involves removing most of the muscles that attach to the back of the jaw and come down on either side of the trachea. It is a massive operation, however, and is only moderately successful.

A simpler method of treatment is to cover the inside of the stall with chicken wire. The sharp chicken wire may discourage the horse from biting and therefore break this habit. Another form of treatment is a cribbing strap (Fig. 51). This is a leather strap about 2½ inches wide that fits over the horse's neck and presses on the throat just behind the horse's cheeks. This treatment is quite successful in some horses.

A Scottish veterinarian has reported some success with a method in which he removes a piece of hide and muscle about the size of a quarter on either cheek 2 inches back from the corner of the mouth. The lining of the mouth is pulled out through the hole and sutured to the skin. A hole is then cut through the lining, making the hole permanent. When the animal grabs onto something in order to suck air, the air comes through the holes instead of through the mouth. This does not satisfy his habit, and the horse will stop cribbing.

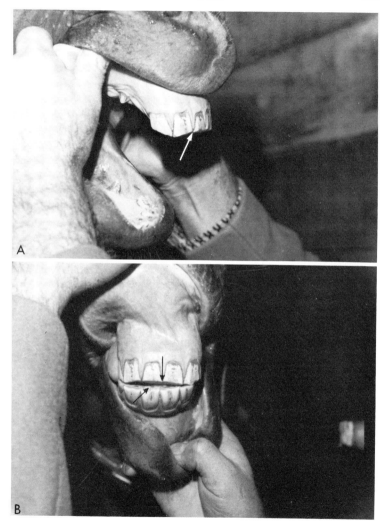

Figure 50

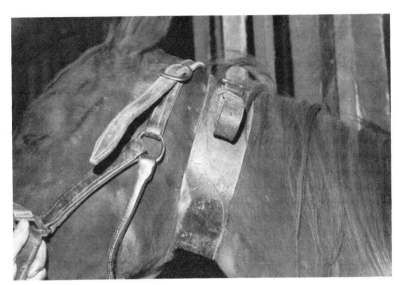

Figure 51

WEAVING

Like cribbing, weaving is a nervous habit. The animal swings his head and neck from side to side. Animals that weave are usually poor feeders and poor doers.

Many ways have been tried to make a horse stop this habit. Some people hang plastic bottles from the ceiling of the stall so the animal will hit them as he moves from side to side. Others hang old car tires in the stall. I think hanging a mirror on the wall of the stall also may stop the horse from weaving.

Horses that have been weaving for a long time will likely never stop. They will stand with their head out the door and will shift their weight from one leg to the other and swing from side to side.

HEAD SHAKING

Head shaking is a nervous disorder much like cribbing. Once this habit has developed it is difficult to break. However, I know of one horse that did stop. The owner put a large stainless steel mirror on the wall. When the horse started to wind his head and walk his stall, he got to the mirror, saw his reflection, and quit.

WOBBLER SYNDROME

Wobbler syndrome is caused by a fracture or narrowing of the spinal cord in the area of the third to the seventh cervical vertebrae. This can be an inherited condition or can result from a direct injury to the neck.

Wobbler syndrome causes a loss of control of the horse's back legs, and to a lesser degree, the front legs. The animal is able to walk a straight line but if his head is turned to one side, he will walk by crossing the back legs. The horse will also swing his back legs away from the body.

The severity of wobbler syndrome may range from bad gait to complete paralysis of the body, which, of course, will ultimately result in death.

Wobbler syndrome usually occurs during one of the growth stages. I see it most often in weanlings, but I have also seen it in 3-year-olds that have been racing for a year. These animals tend to have a bad gait and to drag their toes behind. It becomes more obvious at 4 years of age. Four-year-olds with wobbler syndrome stagger, cross their back legs, and, if they are turned quickly to either the left or right, they will fall down.

An attempt to diagnose this condition by x-ray has met with some success. There has also been some attempt to fix the first and second vertebrae with screwnails to keep them from moving. However, in most cases the screwnails either bend or break. (I am told that this procedure has proved successful in the great dane, however.)

OTHER CONDITIONS CAUSING BAD GAIT

Certain types of lesions may occur along the spinal cord that will give the appearance of wobbler syndrome.

In *brucellosis,* a lesion appears along the spinal cord in the neck region that causes the animal to stagger behind. A blood test can determine if the animal has this condition.

Tuberculosis is another condition that may simulate wobbler syndrome. Although horses are not usually susceptible to tuberculosis, in areas of the world where there is a high incidence of this disease lesions can occur along the spinal cord and produce symptoms that we normally associate with the wobbler syndrome. A tuberculin test can diagnose this problem.

A *fracture to a vertebra just ahead of the pelvis* will cause the animal to become bad gaited behind. An x-ray of the lumbar region will identify this problem.

Strongyles can also cause a horse to become bad gaited behind. (See page 67).

CIRCULATORY DISORDERS

HEART RATE

The normal heart rate (pulse) of a horse is 44 beats per minute. When the animal is racing, however, the rate goes up to 280. An animal in good condition should return to his normal rate about 20 minutes after the race. If the horse takes a much longer period of time to resume the normal rate, this is a good indication that the animal is in poor condition.

Heart rate is significant in certain cases of colic. A heart rate of 60, accompanied by a thready pulse, certainly indicates colic. These symptoms also appear in pneumonia. Other general signs that the heart is not functioning properly are a bluish color in the mouth and congestion of the blood vessels in the eye. These symptoms indicate an interference of blood supply or circulation in the body.

Heart sounds may be significant as an indication of valvular trouble. However, do not be alarmed by the so-called third heart beat. Many healthy animals that are working or racing will have a slight third heart sound.

VEINS

An enlarged vein in the foot or ankle indicates trouble below this area. There may be an abscess in the hoof wall, extensive navicular disease, or infection in the foot due to a nail. The artery next to the enlarged vein will show an extremely strong or throbbing pulse at the ankle (fetlock). Sometimes the large vein that runs up the inside of the back leg will become enlarged and resemble a varicose vein. A drug known as Arlidin (Arlington Funk Laboratories), which comes in a 6 mg tablet (give 8 tablets a day in the feed), will resolve this problem.

Occasionally, a horse with lymphangitis will be mistakenly thought to have varicose veins. In lymphangitis, however, the lymph duct becomes plugged. (See page 120.)

Veins in the hind limbs that fill slowly after exercise are discussed under Parasitic Infestations (see page 67).

SUNSTROKE

When a horse is worked hard under an extremely hot sun, he is subject to sunstroke. This condition is characterized by an extremely high fever (up to 108° F), with no sweating. The animal staggers and will likely go down. If the animal is down by the time help reaches him, he is usually beyond recovery.

Sunstroke is one condition in which too much water is not harmful. If a horse is suffering from sunstroke, pass a tube up the nostril and into the stomach and pump as much cold water as is deemed safe into the stomach. Pass a tube into the rectum and pump as much cold water as possible into this area. Then pack ice cubes around the head, and pour cold water all over the body.

After the treatment described above has been carried out, an antihistamine and a steroid should be injected into the animal. Follow directions on the label as to dosage for each drug. The chance of recovery should be good.

ELEPHANTIASIS
(GREASE LEG)

Elephantiasis occurs when the lymph ducts to the foot become plugged with fibrin, a by-product of low-grade infection. It usually affects the back legs but may be seen in the front limbs. The leg will swell to enormous dimensions and will often appear greasy. The skin on the affected leg becomes quite thick, but the horse will not appear to be very lame.

Elephantiasis is seldom seen today, but it used to be a common problem in work horses. In the early stages of the disease, antibiotics and injectable enzymes can be tried, but as a general rule this treatment has not been very successful.*

Figure 52 shows elephantiasis in a front limb. This case was corrected by injecting enzymes and treating with a daily whirlpool and daily doses of a diuretic. This particular limb did not become greasy.

_____

*Since enzymes are so specialized, they should only be prescribed by a veterinarian.

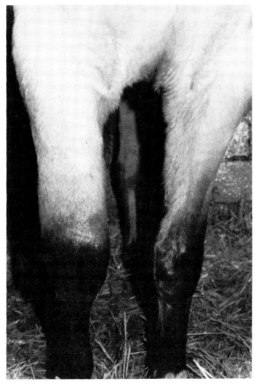

Figure 52

PARTURITION

TESTING FOR PREGNANCY

By rectal palpation the experts that work the big farms can determine whether a mare is pregnant 22 days after she has been bred. Those of us not as experienced prefer to wait about 45 days before checking the mare. The embryo is about the size of a golf ball. The uterus will be firm and round.

If no one is available to do a rectal palpation, then a blood sample taken from 60 to 90 days after breeding should be sent to a veterinary laboratory. The technicians will inject blood serum from the mare into an immature rat. If the rat's uterus is found to be swollen and red at autopsy, then the mare is in foal.

One hundred and twenty-five days after conception, hormones appear in the urine. If a urine sample is sent to the laboratory, the technicians can tell whether or not the mare is in foal. This test can be used from 125 days to seven months after breeding and is known as the *Cuboni test.*

FOALING

In a normal birth, labor is of very short duration. If the mare shows signs of foaling, don't go out for coffee or you'll miss it, since a normal presentation in a healthy mare takes about five minutes.

When the mare lays down, the water breaks and the foal's legs emerge. After three or four contractions, the head appears. One more contraction and the foal is born. The afterbirth usually follows within the hour.

Should the mare have trouble and only one of the foal's feet emerges, send for a veterinarian. However, a good horseman can do much to help the mare before the veterinarian arrives. Wash your hands and arms and reach into the vagina to see whether a foot or the head is turned back. If it is, then straighten it out.

Some people claim that when wax appears on the mare's nipples, the foal is due; however, some mares will wax for as long as 30 days before foaling. Although the duration of the average pregnancy is about 336 days, many mares will carry a foal for as long as a year. Many will go 10 days over term.

Premature Foals

Some mares foal prematurely. Premature foals are difficult to save. If they are born after the tenth month, some can be saved, but they will need a great deal of care and first aid. With time and effort on the part of the owners, these foals will catch up and become healthy, useful animals.

Breech Birth

A breech birth means that the foal's tail presents first. This is a very serious situation, but if you handle it properly, the foal will survive. Remember that the head is inside. Therefore, if the umbilical cord is caught on a back leg it will rupture, and the foal will drown in the amniotic fluids inside the mare. Once the cord breaks, the foal will need to breathe, so speed is important.

Artificial respiration may be necessary if the cord breaks prematurely. Or, if you are strong enough, you can tie ropes to the foal's back legs and spin him around like a centrifuge. This action will cause the fluids to fly out of his mouth.

If the foal dies while inside the mare, it should be cut into pieces and removed. Do not wait. If you delay, the mare will go into shock—she will break out in a cold sweat, her pulse will drop, and the mucous membranes of her mouth and lips of the vulva will turn purple—and die. Covering the mare with blankets and administering large amounts of intravenous fluids may stabilize the blood pressure enough so that the veterinarian can later perform cesarean section and save the mare. Many mares are saved by cesarean section, and they are able to deliver healthy, normal foals in subsequent pregnancies.

Inducing Labor

Some horse owners are tempted to give a mare a hormone shot in order to bring her into labor. The mare may be overdue, and the owners are concerned that she will have trouble giving birth to a large foal. They reason that by giving her a shot they will know exactly when the foal is due and can be prepared by having the veterinarian standing by.

I think this practice is more likely to cause rather than avert trouble. My experience has been that if you give the mare hormones to relax the cervix she will not wait for the cervix to get big enough to pass the colt. She will be down and straining before everything is ready. Once a foot comes down the canal and she gets the message that the foal's to be born, then everything has to work right. If the cervix is not ready and it tears, then you have got trouble.

AFTERBIRTH

After the foal is born, the afterbirth remains attached to the wall of the uterus. The afterbirth is very heavy tissue and will generally drop out of the mare after she stands up. However, mares that do not clean will founder, and they will founder very badly. They will also develop a serious vaginal infection, which can be a real problem. If this happens, it will be difficult to get the mare cleaned up well enough to breed again.

If the afterbirth has not been expelled two hours after foaling, the mare should be helped to clean. The afterbirth should be removed. Since the entire wall of the afterbirth is attached to the uterus, care must be taken that the afterbirth is gently eased away from the uterine wall. The uterus has two horns, and although the foal occupies only one horn during pregnancy, the other horn also has membrane that must be removed. Therefore, when the afterbirth has been eased out, it should be spread on the ground and checked to make sure that there are two blind pouches, one for each horn. If only one pouch is found and there is an open end, then a piece has been left inside the mare. It will probably be too far away to be reached by hand so it must be left to dissolve.

If it has been determined that a piece of the afterbirth still remains in the uterus, then a tablet containing sulfa drugs must be placed inside the uterus to reduce the chance of infection. If the uterus starts to swell and the mare gets a fever, she will founder. You will then have to treat the founder as well as the infection that originally caused the founder.

The foal is still in the sac when it is born. Most mares will reach back and break the sac with their teeth; however, a mare having her first foal may not know enough to break the sac. Many foals have smothered in the afterbirth. This is one reason why someone should be with a mare that is having her first foal. After a mare has had a foal or two, it is probably best to leave her alone.

Some mares tend to get up a little too quickly after foaling, snapping the umbilical cord too long on the foal. When this happens, the cord should be clamped and then cut with sterile scissors.

When a foal is born I always saturate the navel with iodine to prevent *joint ill* (see pages 101 and 153). I like to give the foal 10 ml and the mare 20 ml of penicillin-streptomycin. Since some of the pen-strep passes into the mare's milk, the foal receives, in effect, an extra dose. I also think it is wise to give tetanus shots to both the mare and the foal. This is good first aid and it can prevent many future problems.

BACTERIAL ABORTION

Bacterial abortion may occur at any time during pregnancy, although it usually occurs about 50 to 60 days after conception. Part of the womb becomes infected and part remains healthy. The embryo can live in the healthy environment until it grows large enough to involve the infected part of the womb. At that time, the poison from the infection is absorbed by the foal and it will die. The mare then aborts.

This infection often develops when a mare sucks air into her vagina, or when secretions from the rectum drip into the vagina. Most of the bacteria that cause the infection live in the presence of air. Therefore, if the source of air is removed, the infection will not develop at all or, if present, will disappear.

The Caslick operation, which consists of suturing part of the lips of the vulva together, leaving enough room for the mare to pass her urine, is the time-honored procedure for rectifying this problem. To facilitate healing of the two lips, a small amount of anesthetic is injected at the junction of the skin and mucosa of the vulva (Fig. 53). A thin strip of the mucosa is removed with scissors, and the two edges are sutured together (Fig. 54). Stitches are removed in about three weeks.

Of course, the vulva must be completely open for the mare to be bred and then to foal. After a mare has delivered a foal and the afterbirth, temporary clamps are applied; they are later removed for breeding. The vulva can be sutured again after it has been determined that the mare is in foal.

Mares who have aborted should be checked by a veterinarian. Bacteria from the womb should be cultured so that a proper antibiotic can be administered to kill the infection. This treatment will facilitate a normal pregnancy at a later date.

Some scarring of the uterus may result from the infection. If so, the scar tissue should be scraped away (dilatation and curettage). The veterinarian should then flush the uterus with a baking soda and antibiotic solution.

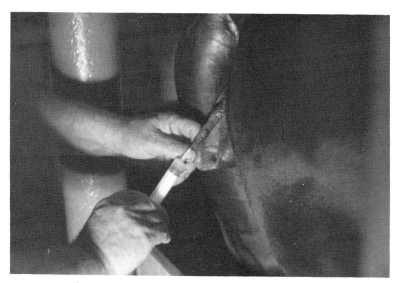

Figure 53

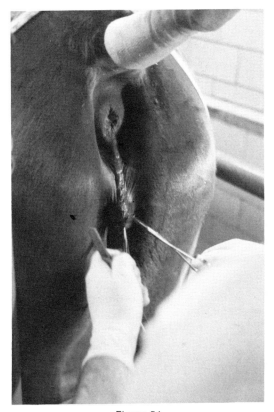

Figure 54

VIRAL ABORTION

There are several types of viral infections that can cause abortions; in fact, a book could be written about this problem alone.

The most common virus responsible for abortion is known as "race track virus." Two- and three-year-olds who have been exposed to this virus return from the track with a cough. Pregnant mares in the same barn as the infected horses will then become infected.

Arteries in the umbilical cord become inflamed and enlarged, a condition that interferes with the blood supply to the foal. As a result, these mares generally abort a live foal that does not survive.

The subject of viral abortion is such a large and complicated one that I think it would be best if the reader referred to virology textbooks or obtained reprints of published articles that are available from the United States Department of Agriculture in Washington, D.C.

Presently rhinopneumonitis virus is the most serious problem for the breeder. It causes high fevers, nasal discharge, and chronic cough in young animals, and abortion in mares. Norden Laboratories has developed an effective vaccine. Consult your veterinarian for a vaccine program.

ABSORPTION

Occasionally a mare will not abort a foal but will absorb it. This generally occurs sometime during the early stages of the pregnancy, between 40 and 60 days.

Absorption is thought to be caused by a systemic infection such as septicemia (blood poisoning) due to a wound. The toxins created by the infection travel through the mare's system and subsequently end the pregnancy.

As a precautionary measure against absorption, it is always a wise policy, once it is established that the mare is pregnant, to check and confirm that the embryo is growing. This can be done most effectively by rectal palpation.

TWINNING

Twinning usually results in two dead foals that are generally born two to three months premature. Occasionally a mare will deliver a normal set of twins but they will not develop into high quality horses. My experience has been that twins do not become strong animals.

Occasionally a mare will have one live and one dead foal, and sometimes one twin will become partially absorbed and be incorporated into the body of the other foal. This is thought to happen because the mare dropped two eggs, both of which were fertilized. One embryo then died and in the process of absorption the dead embryo was caught inside the healthy embryo.

The absorbed twin takes on the character of a deciduous cyst below the ear of the healthy foal. A duct runs along the edge of the ear and when it is squeezed a white fluid with black flecks can be seen. When the cyst is removed, a sac that may contain hair, teeth, and leg bones will be found. The sac may be as small as an egg or as large as a human hand.

MILK FEVER, LACTATING TETANY IN MARES

Although common in the cow, milk fever is rare in horses because, unlike the cow, the mare is able to balance the levels of calcium and phosphorus in her body in the proper ratio so as not to contract lactating tetany.

When milk fever does occur, however, it appears about a week before the mare foals. Symptoms of milk fever are staggering and loss of coordination.

When all other possibilities have been discarded and it has been determined that milk fever is the cause of the symptoms, the mare should be given 250 ml of calcium gluconate intravenously very slowly. One dose will suffice.

The normal free serum calcium and phosphorus levels in a pregnant mare are 3.5 mg of phosphorus and 11.5 mg of calcium per 100 ml of blood. When the serum calcium level drops below 8 mg and the mare staggers, calcium therapy is indicated.

PROBLEMS
IN
THE
NEWBORN

BARKERS (DUMMY FOALS)

These retarded foals are called barkers because they bark like a dog. The probable cause of retardation is lack of oxygen to the brain while the foal was inside the mother.

This condition in the newborn foal is characterized by convulsions, lack of sucking reflex, spasm of the neck muscles, coma, subnormal temperature, and rapid breathing. These symptoms appear during the first 24 hours of life.

Although I have never seen any of these foals survive, intravenous feeding, tranquilizers to reduce spasms, and feeding by a stomach tube would be indicated.

DEFORMED LIMBS

Many foals seem deformed right after they are born, but after three or four weeks they become very good-looking colts. So do not be too concerned because the foal is crooked behind, cannot stand up very well in front, and has to put both knees together when he does stand up; he will probably be all right.

Some foals, however, are born with contracted tendons. They walk on their fetlocks and cannot get their feet on the ground. This problem is congenital, and it is best to put this foal down ("put it to sleep").

If, after six weeks, the front feet are still turned out and the foal tends to stand with both knees together for balance, epiphyseal staples are indicated. These staples allow the outside of the epiphysis at the knee to grow but inhibit the growth at the epiphyseal line at the inside, thus permitting the leg to straighten up and the foot to turn in.

In Figure 55, needles are placed over the epiphyseal line to act as a guide for inserting the epiphyseal staple in the right position. Correct positioning is also confirmed by x-rays. A special instrument is placed on the staple so that one prong can be driven in at a time (Fig. 56).

Figure 57 shows the epiphyseal staple in place.

In Figure 58, the epiphyseal staple is in place to prevent

growth of bone on the medial aspect of the leg. This allows the lateral aspect to grow, thereby bringing the toe around.

The staple is removed several weeks after the foot positioning has been corrected and the foot turns in.

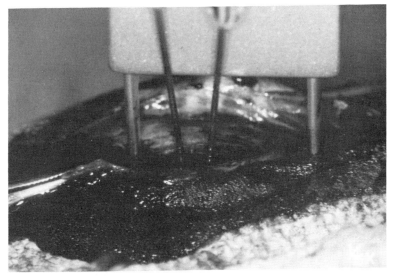

Figure 55

Figure 56

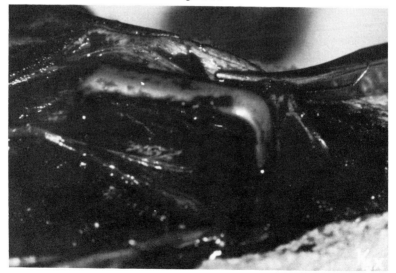

Figure 57

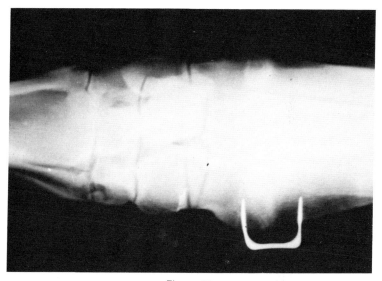

Figure 58

CONSTIPATED FOAL

A constipated foal is a sick foal. A simple way to prevent or cure constipation is to cut a small piece of bar soap so that it is about the size of your little finger, insert this into the rectum. The soap will dissolve and lubricate the rectum, allowing the yellow mucous plug to come out quite easily.

I think it is neither necessary nor safe to insert enema gadgets into the rectum. I once saw a foal die of peritonitis because a large horse thermometer had been inserted in the rectum accidently through the rectum wall.

There is no harm in putting a small piece of soap into the rectum as a suppository.

SCOURING IN FOALS

All foals scour (experience diarrhea) when they are nine days old, since this is the time that the mare comes into her foal heat. The condition is transitory, and many foals are not even treated for it. If treatment is desired, however, just administer a little kalin and pectin combined with a sulfa drug. Any calf scour medicine that a veterinarian normally carries in his bag is suitable for foals with uncomplicated scours.

A foal may get violent scours; it will lose a great amount of fluid, become dehydrated, and die. In this case the veterinarian must give the animal electrolytes intravenously in large quantities in order to save its life. The animal should also be given antibiotics intramuscularly in an attempt to kill the bacteria causing the scours.

In this type of situation there is no time to take cultures to find out which bacteria are responsible; therefore, a good wide-spectrum antibiotic should be used that will be effective against many bacteria. In addition, kalin and pectin should be used to reduce the frequency of bowel movement.

HERNIAS

Umbilical Hernias

Occasionally, foals are born with small umbilical hernias. A good rule to follow as far as treatment is concerned is that if you can put your thumb through the hole, the hernia should be repaired.

If the hernia is as big as your thumb, then as the foal grows the hole will get larger. The danger is that a piece of gut could get into the sac and strangulate, and the animal would die of peritonitis. Therefore, if you can get your thumb into the umbilical hernia, have the hernia repaired when the foal is four to five months of age.

Scrotal Hernias

Watch for scrotal hernias in stud colts.

If the colt has a scrotal sac the size of that of a normal yearling instead of a newborn foal, test to see if the intestine is down in the sac. Squeeze the scrotum and feel the intestine inside. It will move up into the belly. If you find that the intestine *is* in the sac, the hernia must be repaired almost immediately.

As long as the foal remains on milk he will probably experience little difficulty because his manure will not be solid. However, once he gets into his mother's grain and starts nibbling on grass his manure will become harder, and that part of the intestine that falls into the cavity will strangulate and the foal will die. Therefore, the hernia must be repaired before the foal's manure becomes hard.

If you do not want to remove a testicle from a colt with a scrotal hernia, a screen may be inserted instead. It is not difficult to do. A ring can be made so that the cord to the testicle can pass through the screen.

INVERTED EYELIDS
(ENTROPION)

Entropion, seen most often in foals, is an inversion of the margin of the eyelids, usually the bottom lid. The animal suffering from entropion has a chronic eye infection and tearing caused by the eyelashes rubbing against the cornea.

Treatment of entropion consists of cutting a small V-shaped piece of skin from the bottom of the lid. When the incision heals, the skin contracts, thus keeping the lid from curling back into the eye. The eye should then be bathed with boracic acid solution followed by a suitable antibiotic eye ointment. Do not use a steroid, since it will inhibit healing.

HEMOLYTIC JAUNDICE IN FOALS

Hemolytic jaundice is characterized by a yellowish color of the inner part of the foal's eyelids and lips. In the filly, the vulva will also be yellow in color.

While she is pregnant, the mare builds up a resistance to her foal. When the foal sucks the mother's milk, antibodies in the colostrum (first milk) attack the red blood cells in the foal, causing their destruction. This condition is similar to the Rh blood factor in humans.

A jaundiced foal must have his blood changed immediately. Drain as much of the foal's blood as you deem safe and replace it with blood from a donor horse that is unrelated to the mother. The foal must also be put on a nurse mare. If one cannot be found, a product called "Foal-lac" may be used instead.

I know of several cases in which nurse mares were not available and the foals were raised by goats. The foal sucks the goat as though it were its mother. The goat may have to stand on a couple of straw bales so that the foal can reach her. Be sure to use a goat that will not dry up in a few weeks because if another goat is brought in, the foal may get diarrhea as a result of the change.

Jaundice may be prevented by taking blood samples from the mare and stallion and having them typed at a laboratory. If a foal is born with jaundice, rebreed the mare to a stallion that is completely unrelated to the one that fathered the jaundiced foal.

SINUS INFECTION IN FOALS

Some poorly ventilated barns seem to be havens for infections affecting the foal's sinus. On the third or fourth day of life, the foal may have such a bad nasal discharge that you may think he is going to develop distemper, but it is usually nothing more than a ventilation problem.

The foal should be given an antibiotic and put in the fresh air. Penicillin-streptomycin should clear up the problem. If that combination does not work, a wide-spectrum antibiotic (e.g., chloramphenicol) should be used.

The mother should be treated as well. She may have a mild infection, although there will not be much nasal discharge.

PNEUMONIA IN THE FOAL

If a foal is born outside in the rain, it can acquire a true case of pneumonia unrelated to joint ill. This pneumonia responds to almost any antibiotic, such as penicillin-streptomycin. Other pneumonias are caused by Actinobacillus organisms, formerly known as Shigella, and *Streptococcus equi.*

The Streptococcus–joint ill complex becomes apparent about two weeks after birth. The pneumonia may appear first, with rapid breathing and high temperature; swollen joints occur later. If the complex is chronic in nature, the stifle and ankles swell first. Then, when the animal is debilitated, *Streptococcus equi* invade the lungs and cause a true pneumonia. This also responds to treatment with antibiotics as discussed under the heading Kidney Infection (see page 101).

Shigellosis, or actinobacillosis, is characterized by an extremely rapid onset. The foal is apparently normal when born, but after 12 to 24 hours it becomes prostate, with heavy breathing and high temperature. It usually dies before any antibiotic can take effect. This type of pneumonia is thought to be contracted or inherited while the foal is in the uterus. The mare may be a carrier without demonstrating the disease.

To differentiate these types of pneumonia, it is necessary to culture lung tissue from the dead foal.

Another type of pneumonia is found only in the Arabian

horse. The foals are normal when born and then develop the classic signs of rapid breathing and high temperature; however, they do not respond to antibiotics. Death follows about two weeks after birth.

The causative agent is an adenovirus. The effect of this virus on the foal is extreme because the Arabian horse is born without a certain immunity process. These horses lack gamma globulin, an antibody responsible for the immunity against this type of disease.

Since this type of pneumonia is an inherited condition, the only solution is not to breed the mother of an affected foal back to the same stallion. I know of one Arabian mare that produced two foals with an adenovirus when she was bred to the same stallion. When she was bred to another stallion, she had a normal foal.

POISONING

AMMONIA POISONING

Ammonia poisoning may occur when the animal licks fertilizer bags. If the animal develops severe colic and perhaps some diarrhea, and has had access to fertilizer bags, even empty ones, there is a very strong possibility that he is suffering from ammonia poisoning.

The treatment of choice is to give the adult horse a gallon of mineral oil to soothe the stomach. (A young horse or pony will take a relatively smaller amount of mineral oil.) Intravenous administration of methylene blue or a similar dye preparation will capture the ammonia, and it will then be excreted.

ARSENIC POISONING

Arsenic is a cumulative drug, and a horse can tolerate large amounts of it. However, the body gets rid of it at a very slow rate. The source of the arsenic is usually bran or other grains that have been treated with a Paris green preparation used to kill cutworms.

The symptoms of arsenic poisoning vary a great deal, depending upon the amount ingested. Small amounts of arsenic in excess of what can be normally tolerated produce an unthrifty condition — swollen joints, slight colic, and so forth. Large amounts of arsenic cause violent diarrhea, a staggering gait, severe colic pains, poor circulation, and so on.

Most horses are smart enough not to eat grains treated with arsenic. I have been on farms where cattle have died from eating treated grains but the horses were healthy. They were smarter than the cows and left the grain alone.

Arsenic poisoning may be treated by injecting British anti-lewisite (BAL) intramuscularly. When the animal is given the recommended dosage (as printed on the label), his recovery is spectacular.

FERN POISONING

The young fern plant is poisonous only when it is emerging from the stem and before the leaf is formed. Fern, or bracken, poisoning causes blood to appear in the manure and urine.

Treatment includes removing the animal from the fern area and administering blood transfusions. A gallon of mineral oil given orally will flush the animal's digestive system.

LEAD POISONING

Lead poisoning in the horse may cause a stilty gait or may even result in paralysis and death. When a horse with lead poisoning walks, he will jerk his limbs and head and flick his eyes. However, these symptoms should not be confused with those of tetanus or rabies.

If you notice that a horse is walking with this jerking action, check his stall; you will probably find an old paint can or an old door that was once covered with a lead-based paint. I once saw an animal die because he had licked an area not much bigger than a quarter on an old door.

Lead poisoning often occurs in ponies that are kept as pets in paddocks made of old boards and doors. If they chew boards covered with lead paint, they will develop lead poisoning.

Calcium levulinate is the recognized treatment and should be injected slowly into the blood stream. This will cause the lead to form an insoluble salt that is readily excreted through the kidneys. A gallon of mineral oil should be given to the adult horse to cleanse the digestive system.

STRYCHNINE POISONING

Strychnine is an extract of *nux-vomica*, the seeds of a tree grown in the West Indies, and tincture of *nux-vomica* is the standard ingredient in an appetizer for large animals. I once saw a case of strychnine poisoning on a farm where the owner was using strychnine on corn to kill crows, but his horse ate the corn instead.

The horse suffering from strychnine poisoning will go into convulsions and pull his head straight back. A snap of the fingers or a loud noise will make the animal convulse.

The convulsions are similar to an epileptic seizure: The tail is kinked back, the jaws are very tight, and the legs are straight and tense. The horse will relax for a short period of time and then will go into another convulsion.

A large dose of strychnine will paralyze the muscles that control breathing and the animal will die from lack of oxygen.

When strychnine poisoning does occur, tranquilizers are recommended to keep the animal as quiet as possible. Do not touch him until you are prepared to treat him. If there are no severe convulsions, purge him with mineral oil. In an effort to relax the spasms, intravenous anesthetics such as barbiturates or chloral hydrate (chloral butanol) should be administered. Once the animal starts to sleep the danger period is over.

DIABETES

In horses, this problem is actually classified as an insulin deficiency rather than as diabetes, as it is described in humans. The animal cannot burn sugar as it becomes available.

A diabetic horse generally has a rough hair coat. He carries too much weight and has too much stomach, regardless of how much work he does. He does not work or race well and is usually dull rather than hyper. He also has a tendency to drink large quantities of water.

The blood sugar level may be within the normal range (about 60 to 100 mg per 100 ml of blood) while the animal is at rest; however, if a 20 per cent solution of glucose (based on 4 gm per kg of body weight) is pumped by stomach tube into the horse and a series of blood sugar level tests is made at 30 minutes, 60 minutes, 120 minutes, and so on, it will be found that the animal will not be able to metabolize the sugar as quickly as he normally should.

To correct the situation and establish the proper insulin dosage, pump a 20 per cent solution of glucose (based on 4 gm per kg of body weight) into the horse the following day, then administer insulin. Perform the series of tests again at 30, 60, 120 minutes, and so on. These tests will show that when the animal was supplied with insulin he was able to utilize sugar more efficiently. Therefore, it must be assumed that the animal has an insulin deficiency.

In most cases this condition is transitory. Once the horse becomes regulated with a given dosage of insulin, he can be slowly weaned from it and will return to normal without the need of daily shots for the rest of his life.

In order to reverse insulin deficiency, I have administered up to 300 international units of aqueous insulin. The next day I was able to reduce this level by one third and still maintain the animal in good health. As research on the sugar balance of the horse continues and knowledge on the subject increases, I believe that insulin will become a required nutrient for some working animals.

In the past it was routine to give some horses one-half liter of a 50 per cent solution of glucose the day before a race. It did improve performance in certain instances, but sometimes an owner or trainer would come back to me and say, "Doc, you put my horse to sleep. He didn't race well." The key to this complaint was that the horse did not need extra glucose, he needed extra insulin.

SWAMP FEVER (EQUINE INFECTIOUS ANEMIA)

Swamp fever is a debilitating disease characterized by a rapid drop in the number of red corpuscles in the blood. The horse with swamp fever has edema, or swelling, of the stomach and legs and jaundice-like lesions in the mouth and around the eyes. Although appetite remains good, the horse experiences a rapid loss of weight and, in some cases, death occurs in a few days.

This disease is spread by blood-sucking insects such as the mosquito and the black fly; thus, it is prevalent in those areas where mosquitoes and black flies are numerous. In Florida and Louisiana, for example, it is endemic because of the mosquitos, and in northern and eastern Canada it is carried by the black fly and the green-headed horse fly.

Swamp fever can be diagnosed by the Coggins test. Many American states, as well as the Canadian government, have implemented testing programs in an attempt to eliminate this disease. As a result, swamp fever is not as common as it once was, and I think it will eventually disappear entirely.

I believe that, in addition to the bite of the insect that carries the disease, there must be physical contact with an affected horse in order for the disease to spread. There have been instances in which nearly all the horses on one farm had swamp fever while the herd on the farm on the other side of the fence was entirely free of the disease. Very seldom do stallions contract swamp fever, because they are usually kept in the barn and rarely have contact with the other horses.

Some horses that have contracted swamp fever and then recovered have become immune carriers. These animals can race or work normally; however, if they are turned out with a herd of susceptible horses, the disease will be transmitted.

Another common carrier of swamp fever is the dirty hypodermic needle. This, I believe, is the way the disease is spread in the barn. If the needle has been used on an affected horse and then used on a susceptible horse, the animal will contract the disease.

It has been found experimentally that a stallion with a high level of infectious anemia virus in his system was able to infect susceptible mares. The virus was isolated in his semen.

Mares with a high level of virus in their systems and carrying a foal at the time of their death apparently passed on the disease to the foal.

Mares that were not sick but tested positive with the Coggins test had foals that also tested positive. After being isolated from their mothers for a time, these foals later tested negative.

TUBERCULOSIS

Tuberculosis is so rare in the horse that it is practically nonexistent. Horses running with tubercular cattle do not contract the disease.

LYMPHANGITIS (STOCKING UP)

As a result of a low-grade infection in the lower hind limb, the lymph ducts, which are a means of returning fluid to the heart, become plugged. The infection travels through the lymph ducts and infects the lymph nodes along this channel. Whenever a lymph duct is plugged, swelling will occur.

If the lymph ducts are completely clogged, the surrounding tissue becomes extremely susceptible to bacterial growth. The bacteria cause ulcers to form along the line of the lymph ducts starting at the hoof head and progressing up the inside of the back leg. This condition is called *ulcerative lymphangitis*.

Treatment consists of applying hot and cold water compresses or a hot and cold whirlpool bath over the affected area. Potassium iodide in the recommended dosages should be given in the feed. Certain enzymes can be injected into the animal to help dissolve the fibrous material that is formed as a result of blockage in the lymph ducts.

Zinc is a great healer for this type of problem; zinc lotion makes a good dressing, and white lotion is as good as any. Gauze soaked in zinc lotion should be wrapped around the infected area and a bandage should be wrapped around the gauze.

Once the lymph ducts are cleared, the ulcers will heal automatically, since the body has the ability to absorb the debris that originally caused the plugging.

Diuretics such as Lasix (Hoescht-Roussel) would also help.

TETANUS (LOCKJAW)

Tetanus affects all animals, including man. It is mildly contagious; however, usually only one horse in the field or barn will contract tetanus.

Clostridium tetani is the bacterium that causes tetanus. It is an *anaerobe,* a germ that can live without oxygen. *Clostridium tetani* lives in the soil, and its spores enter the body of an animal through a dirty wound. The wound then closes over, thus protecting the organism from oxygen. (For example, this may happen when a horse steps on a contaminated nail.) In the absence of oxygen the tetanus spores become active. *Clostridium tetani* then begin to grow and secrete a strong toxin that travels through the body. Some fields carry this germ in the soil, while others do not. Therefore, some farms will lose a horse every few years from this disease, while other farms will never have a problem.

When a horse does contract tetanus, the first muscles that are affected are those that are most used — the jaw muscles; this is why the disease is commonly known as *lockjaw* — the animal cannot open its mouth. The toxin released by *Clostridium tetani* stimulates the nerves in the muscles, causing them to contract. The animal cannot relax these muscles.

The neck is affected next. The horse with tetanus always stands with his jaw ahead and with an extremely rigid neck. The next muscle involved controls the tail; it becomes cocked parallel to the spine. The shoulders are then affected; the animal will take on a stilty appearance as he stands. Next the hip muscles become rigid. When the disease reaches the hip muscles, the horse will fall over. If he can be lifted somehow, he will probably stand.

A downed horse with tetanus is a dead horse. There are just too many muscle groups affected for the horse to survive. Eventually, the diaphragm becomes involved, and the animal will suffocate.

In the early stages of tetanus the observant groom or owner may recognize certain symptoms. The animal will be stilty looking and will hold his head extended slightly. If he becomes excited, the third eyelid will move halfway across the eye, and it will not return to normal until a few seconds have passed. At this point in the disease the animal is still able to eat.

About 50 per cent of animals with early cases of tetanus can be saved. If they can be kept alive until the fourteenth day after they have contracted the disease, then chances of survival are excellent.

Tranquilization in early tetanus is important so that the horse does not develop convulsions. My experience has been that Sparine (Wyeth), in dosages varying from 5 to 30 ml, depending on the degree of infection, is a specific treatment for tetanus.

The animal should be kept in a relaxed state, so it may be necessary to administer tranquilizers three or four times a day. He should also be placed in a quiet, dark stall where there will be no noise to panic or annoy him.

Sometimes the wound that permitted the spore to enter the animal cannot be found. If the horse is still in the early stages of the disease, pare out the feet and look for a nail hole. Recently, I encountered a fatal case of tetanus in a mare who had only a skin abrasion on the knee. She had broken loose, run into a farm implement, and grazed the side of her knee.

If you are able to locate the wound, clean it, dig it out, make it bleed, do anything to get the area drained. *Clostridium tetani* is an *anaerobe* and cannot live with *oxygen*. Therefore, if you can get oxygen into the wound, the bacteria will die. The death of the bacteria will prevent any more toxin from going through the system.

Some veterinarians prescribe large doses of penicillin, and this treatment does have some merit because the animal may have a fever. However, if a large dose of penicillin excites the animal, then it would be wrong to give it to him. Although one of your first instincts would be to run an intravenous electrolyte into the animal, this could excite him and thus it would be wrong.

If the horse's jaws start to lock, then he can learn to suck gruel. Boil some oats and bran and pour off the liquid. The horse will take it. I have seen horses that would eat 24 eggs a day in a gruel by sucking until they got it all down. Most of these animals are in good flesh and can take two weeks of a very sparse diet.

The best prevention is to have your horse vaccinated with a tetanus toxoid once a year. Tetanus antitoxin (1500 units) gives temporary, immediate immunity and should be given freely when any wounds appear.

Although I do not think that contagiousness is a serious problem for the person handling the affected horse, it is a wise precaution to make sure your own immunity to tetanus is high.

CASTRATION

Most colts are castrated as yearlings. Spring is the best time of the year for this procedure because the grass is green and the flies are at a minimum; these conditions keep the swelling down. If it is necessary to castrate a colt at any other time of the year, he should be given injections of antibiotics continuously for three or four days following castration, and he should have clean bedding and regular exercise.

When a colt is castrated, a two-clamp system is used on the colt to insure minimum hemorrhage (Fig. 59). All too often, however, castrations are done in haste. As a result, the cord may be left too long and will attach itself to the skin, causing a *scirrhous cord* (Fig. 60). A scirrhous cord is a fibrous enlargement of the cord that becomes infected, discharging a white purulent material. This condition will persist for years if the enlargement is not surgically removed.

Sometimes the end of the cord will produce a tumor-like mass that has many weeping sinuses. (Fig. 61). More often, the cord that is left long will adhere to the skin and will enlarge to about 1 inch in diameter in the inguinal ring. Although the growth will not become infected, it will interfere with the horse's gait. A rectal examination will reveal a pronounced pulse in the inguinal ring. As in the case of a scirrhous cord, these growths should be removed surgically.

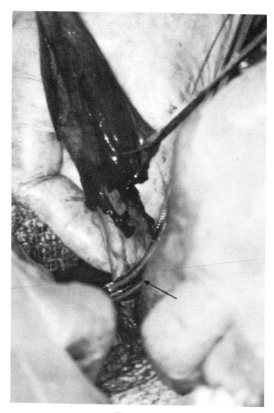

Figure 59

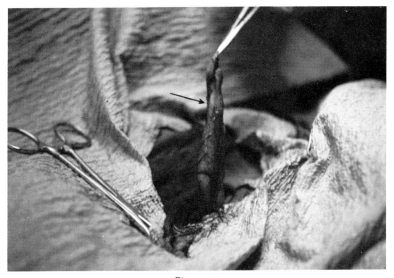

Figure 60

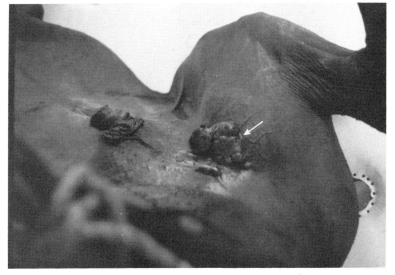

Figure 61

RIDGLINGS, HIGH FLANKERS, RIG CRYPTORCHIDS

Ridglings, high flankers, and rig cryptorchids are colts that have retained one or two testes in the abdominal cavity. These animals should be castrated, as I believe the condition is inherited. Most ridglings are operated on under a general anesthetic, and the normal procedure for castration is used.

The incision is made over the inguinal ring, and a careful search is made along its edge. Some testicular material will be evident. If this is grasped with a pair of forceps, it will lead to the testicle. There is no need to make a great, gaping wound in the abdomen.

In most cases the testicle will be small (about the size of a man's thumb). and the epididymis will be separated from it. Make sure that it is recovered before the castration begins.

Should the ring be more than two fingers wide, an attempt should be made to close it with number four catgut.

ARTIFICIAL
EYE

When a horse loses his eye as a result of an injury or a tumor (Fig. 62), he will accept an artificial one (Fig. 63) that can be removed easily when he is not performing (Fig. 64).

Care must be taken to preserve the tear duct and the third eyelid. Small pieces of fascia from the hip or leg can be folded and sutured to the muscles. The eyelids are sutured together until the collagenous mass fills about half of the orbit. Occasionally, the lower eyelid must be reinforced with a small

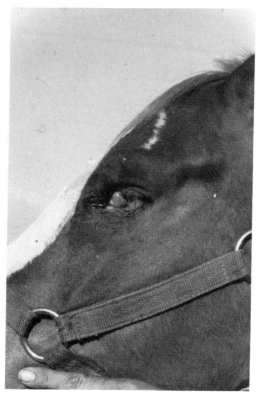

Figure 62

piece of fascia in order to prevent the artificial eye from falling out.

Any manufacturer of plastic eyes for humans will make one for a horse.

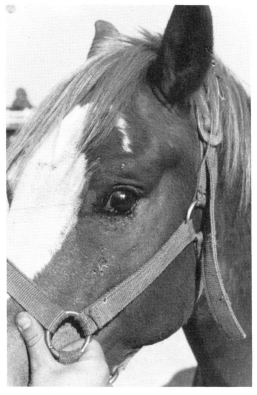

Figure 63

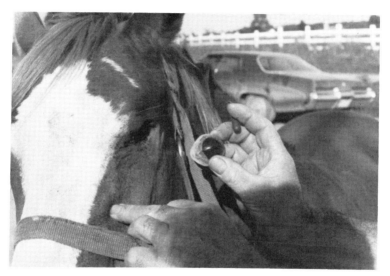

Figure 64

SKIN GRAFTS

Wounds can be healed by skin grafts. The horse in Figure 65 was hurt in a trailer accident.

The leg was conservatively treated with zinc oxide solutions under a bandage until the wound granulated (Fig. 66).

Excessive granulation is surgically removed to below the skin edge (Fig. 67).

Small pinch grafts are removed from the chest (Fig. 68). As

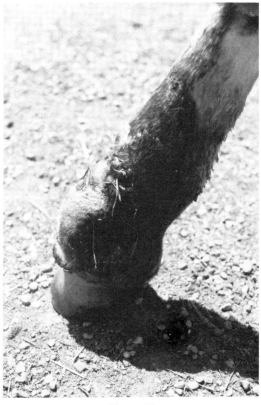

Figure 65

many as 100 grafts are used in a large wound. These pinches are buried in the granulating tissue. Most of the pinch grafts will live and grow, and in time the leg will have a normal growth of hair.

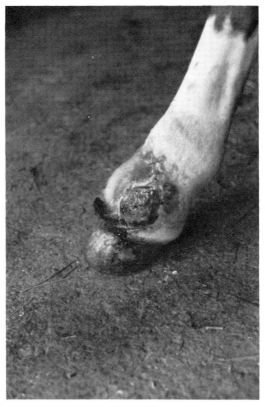

Figure 66

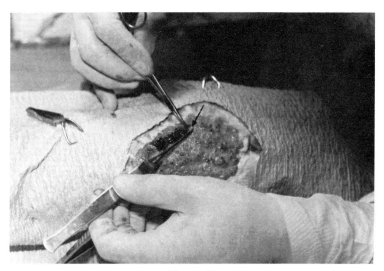

Figure 67

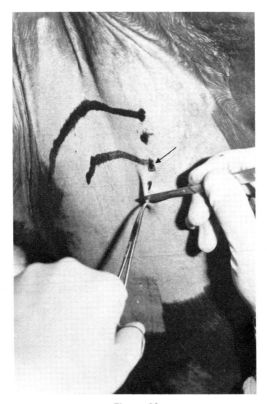

Figure 68

FOOT
PROBLEMS

BRUISES, CORNS, AND CANKERS

Corns at the junction of the wall and the bar of the foot (Fig. 69) are probably one of the most common foot problems causing lameness.

It is thought that most corns are due not to a bruise on the bottom of the foot but to the horse crossfiring or interfering and hitting his quarters in front with a back foot, causing a slight bruise in the wall of the hoof. The bruised material visible after you have dug the foot out is probably the bottom of a bruised wall. You can usually dig quite deep into the sole of the hoof before all the bruised material is removed.

Many times a corn will spread over to the frog and will have the appearance of proud flesh. This type of corn, called a *canker,* may involve part of the frog as well as the sole. It is possible, however, to have a bruised frog and a bruised sole without canker or corn development. Blood streaks can be seen in the bruised sole as you trim it out. Occasionally, the frog will become bruised; this is difficult to diagnose in a dark-colored frog, but as you pare the bruise away it will be pink.

In order to treat these three conditions, you must establish drainage by paring around the bruise or corn area. I prefer to

Figure 69

place about six small pieces of iodine crystal on the corn or bruised sole and then flood the area with oil of turpentine. This creates a blue smoke that cauterizes the small blood vessels leading to the affected area (Fig. 70). Figure 71 shows how the foot will appear after the bruise or corn has been cauterized.

Regarding the canker, it is best to dry the proud flesh–like material with an equal mixture of copper sulfate, zinc sulfate,

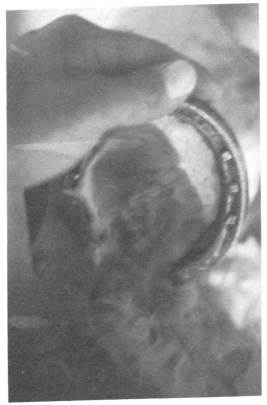

Figure 70

and lead acetate. I usually use about 1 ounce of each dissolved in 16 ounces of water.

Clean the foot thoroughly. Pour the mixture onto some absorbent cotton and tape the cotton to the foot. If this routine is performed daily, the foot will quickly grow underneath, and the canker will dry up and fall off.

Figure 71

THRUSH

Thrush is probably the most common foot problem seen in horses (Fig. 72). It usually occurs in the cleft of the frog and may be detected by its odor, which is very distinctive.

Thrush is a fungal infection that thrives where there is no air. If the frog is not properly trimmed out and is allowed to overlap onto the sole, a space will be created where no air can penetrate. Juices from the stall will work into this area, thus providing a beautiful medium in which the fungus can grow.

Thrush can become complicated when it works its way into the *navicular bursa* (a small bursa between the navicular bone and the flexor tendon that is immediately under the frog; Figure 73). I have also seen extreme cases in which the fungus worked its way up the inside of the hoof wall and exited at the coronet band.

Treatment consists of trimming the frog back so that there are no blind spaces in the foot in which the fungus can grow. In addition, I like to use a mixture of 1 ounce of copper sulfate, 1 ounce of lead acetate, and 1 ounce of zinc sulfate in 16 ounces of water. Shake well, then flood the hoof. Dam the heel with mud so that a pool of medicine can be established. Allow the medicine to soak in for two minutes, then let the foot down (Fig. 74).

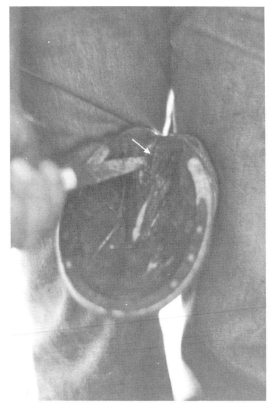

Figure 72

Do this daily. The stall should be kept clean, and lime should be spread over the floor.

    If this treatment plan does not stop the infection from re-curring, spread 10 inches of clean sand or clay on the floor of the stall.

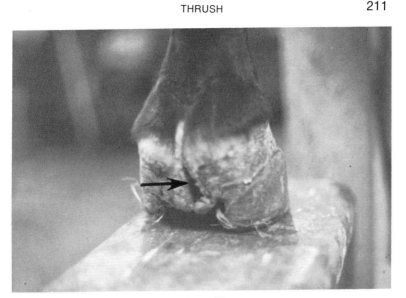

Figure 73

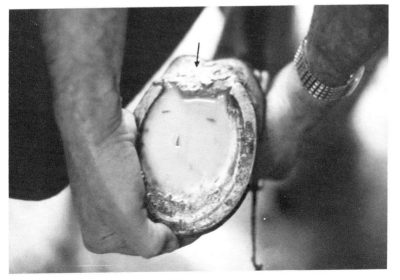

Figure 74

SEEDY TOE

Seedy toe is a small separation in the toe. The area is easily trimmed out with the curled part of a hoof knife. Often the foot will split slightly in the front. Usually this means that at one time the horse had a slight founder.

There is no treatment. The foot will eventually grow out, and the separation will disappear.

QUARTERCRACKS (SPLITS IN THE HOOF)

A quartercrack may be the end result of a corn or a bruised wall. The crack usually starts at the coronet band about 2 inches from the heel (Fig. 75). Figure 76 demonstrates an old chronic case involving the whole quarter. Fresh blood oozes from the crack the first few days. Later, as the wall separates and the blood liquefies, a black fluid will drain through the crack. This is a sign of infection, and the resultant pressure from inside the wall will make the animal hopelessly lame. In Figure 77, the infection involves the coffin bone.

The best treatment is to remove that quartercrack wall surgically (Fig. 78). The area should then be washed with an astringent solution such as I recommend for the treatment of a canker (see p. 206). After a few days the infection should clear up.

When the infection has cleared, place a quartercrack patch over the area. This type of patch is generally made out of an acrylic material (Fig. 79). It will grow down with the wall as the

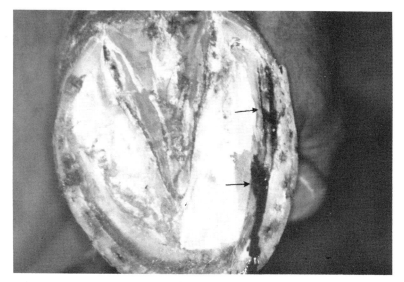

Figure 75

Figure 76

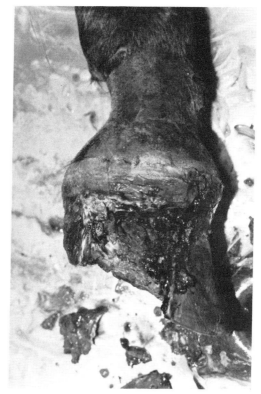

Figure 77

new foot grows. The farrier can nail through the patch if the animal has to be shod.

As an alternative method of treatment, sulfanilamide powder may be applied daily until the infection clears up (Fig. 80). It takes about a year for the hoof to grow out.

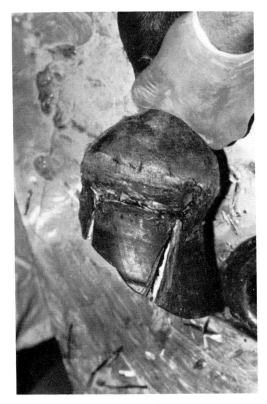

Figure 78

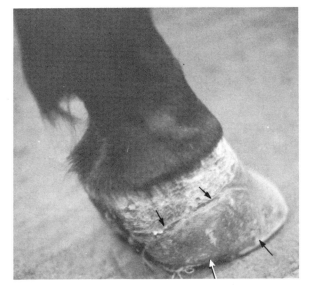

Figure 79

Figure 80

SANDCRACK

A sandcrack differs from a quartercrack in that a sandcrack starts at the junction of the corner of the hoof and the frog. There is no separation between the sole and the wall (Fig. 81). It will come back to the soft part of the heel and will probably involve the frog. Usually a black, thrush-like material is secreted in which a fungus can grow.

In this situation you must first establish drainage. Then soak the area with an astringent solution such as that used for the treatment of a canker (see p. 206). This treatment will kill the infection and the foot will become healthy.

Figure 81

CRACKED HEEL

When a lesion just below the hair at the back of the fetlock at the hoof head excretes a yellow pus, the condition is known as cracked heel. Scabs form, break, and bleed, and the leg swells. This condition may affect one leg or all four legs and can spread to other horses.

Generally the lesion is the result of unsanitary conditions, but it may also be caused by the chemicals used on race tracks to lay the dust or stop freezing. These chemicals predispose the animal to heel cracks; a fungal infection then sets in, and the animal may become very ill.

In the early stages, cracked heel can be controlled by simple, good hygiene. Scrub the animal's ankles with iodine soap, dry them with alcohol, and then apply any suitable antibiotic salve, preferably one that contains a fungicide.

If the problem is longstanding, it may affect the tendons. I have even seen this kind of infection involve the digital sheath and produce large ankles. If this happens, large doses of antibiotics are required, and in most cases the animal will recover in about a week.

FOUNDER (LAMINITIS)

A horse with founder gives the impression that he is anchored to the ground. He does not want to move forward or backward. If he backs, he will slide his feet. The foundered horse walks by placing his heel down first, then his toe; therefore, he walks heel-toe. The horse with navicular disease, on the other hand, walks toe-heel (see p. 227).

Founder primarily affects the front feet; however, I once saw a case in which all four feet had foundered. The front feet of a horse with founder point out, and as a result the horse's chest has a hollow appearance.

The true pathological problem in founder is that the coffin bone drops away from the hoof. This may occur as quickly as 12 hours after the first symptoms of acute founder appear.

Chronic founder is easily diagnosed by x-rays. Instead of the coffin bone being parallel to the wall of the hoof, the toe of the coffin bone is tipped down towards the sole. The space between the wall of the hoof and the coffin bone is filled with blood or fibrin which was deposited by the blood.

In Figure 82, note that the coffin bone has partially rotated. The toe of the coffin bone is farther from the wall of the hoof than it is higher up in the foot. The bone should be parallel to the wall of the hoof. Prognosis is good in this case.

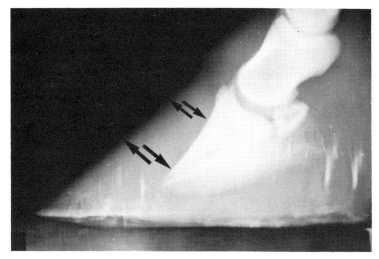

Figure 82

In Figure 83, the coffin bone has rotated to the degree that the point of the bone has penetrated the sole. Prognosis is poor in this case.

The horse shown in Figure 84 has foundered and has an abscessed wall (indicated by the dark space, which is full of pus, at the front of the hoof).

Figure 85 shows the deterioration of the coffin bone due to a longstanding abscess of the foot.

The sequence of events leading up to this change in the position of the coffin bone is not clearly known, but it is known that if the horse eats an excessive amount of grain, he will founder. Founder has been experimentally produced in ponies by feeding them large quantities of corn starch. They develop enteritis (a toxemia) and founder. A horse with an empty stomach that is then turned out onto a lush pasture can overeat and founder. (This syndrome is called *grass founder* and is more common in the pony than in any other breed.)

In addition to overeating, other conditions may cause a horse to founder. A mare that does not get rid of the afterbirth after foaling will develop a temperature and founder. I have also seen founder in horses with high fevers caused by heat strokes.

Acute founder can be produced experimentally by pumping large quantities of corn starch into the animal's stomach. The huge amounts of corn starch change the bacterial flora to the extent that enterotoxins and histamines are produced. These toxins affect the circulatory system, especially in the feet. As a result of this circulatory interference, the tissue that con-

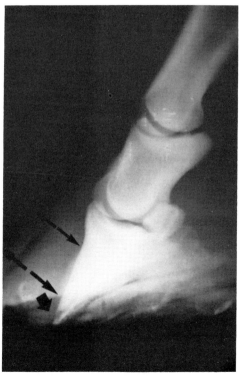

Figure 83

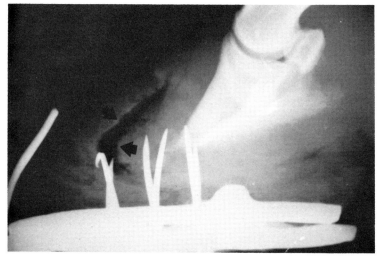

Figure 84

nects the bony foot to the hoof breaks down, allowing the foot to drop away from the wall.

Treatment, whether of acute or chronic founder, is based on reducing inflammation. In many cases, a maximum dose of antihistamine and a large dose of steroid given each day for a period of three days will relieve the condition. Butazolidin (Geigy) given for 10 days will alleviate many of the symptoms. Lasix (Hoechst-Roussel) given once a day for three days is also helpful.

The animal will have a hollow space between the wall of the hoof and the coffin bone, but as the new hoof grows down it will rejoin the coffin bone. This will take 8 to 10 months.

Usually the heel will grow faster than the toe; therefore, the heel will have to be trimmed regularly so that the animal can stand in a comfortable position. Sometimes it is necessary to x-ray the foot to see if the bottom of the coffin bone is parallel to the floor. If it is not, the foot should be trimmed in an attempt to bring this about.

If the toe of the coffin bone comes through the sole, infection will get under the wall and the animal will become very lame. A horse with this type of infection is difficult to save. In most of these cases euthanasia is the kindest thing you can do for the animal.

In the past few years I have been cutting the wall off and replacing it with either plaster of paris or some of the newer

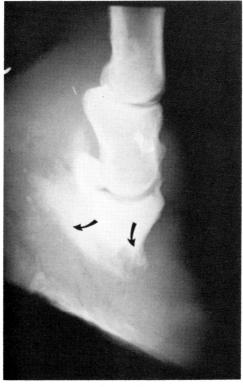

Figure 85

acrylics. I have saved a few top show horses in this way. The new hoof will grow down at the same angle to the coffin bone so that in about a year the animal will be reasonably sound.

Since larges doses of corn starch tend to founder a horse, it is certainly feasible that insulin and thyroid extract are two drugs that should aid in the treatment of the foundered horse.

In summation, use antihistamines and steroids to get the heat out of the feet. If necessary, stand the animal in a mixture of moist warm clay and Epsom salts. In the case of overeating, purge the horse with mineral oil to remove the source of the trouble. Shoe the animal at the angle where he will be the most comfortable.

It is necessary to encourage the hoof to grow at the fastest rate possible. I believe that venous turpentine painted around the hoof head will encourage growth. Two ounces of gelatin a day in the feed seems to improve the quality of the hoof.

D and L Methionine, a precursor to cysteine, which is the precursor to keratin (hoof material), given daily for a few weeks, is also indicated. Twenty-five grams is an arbitrary dose.

A recent study has shown that blocking the nerves to the feet with a local anesthetic that does not contain epinephrine relaxes the blood vessel walls and thus improves the blood flow in a horse with acute founder.

A horse that has foundered will re-founder more easily than one that has not foundered.

NAVICULAR DISEASE

Navicular disease is a broad classification of an arthritic condition involving the navicular bone in the foot and also the bursa between the bone and the tendon. A *bursa* is an oil sac that supplies lubrication between two moving surfaces. Not all horses have a bursa between the tendon and the navicular bone. When this arthritic condition occurs in the foot, the bottom of the navicular bone becomes notched, the tendon passing over these notches becomes irritated, and lameness results. These notches can be seen on x-ray plates. In Figure 86 the small arrow indicates notching of the distal border of the navicular bone, and the large arrows indicate sidebones. Figure 87 shows notching of the distal border (*long arrow*). The short arrow is not pointing out a fracture; the technician left a stone in the foot.

The horse with navicular disease will point his foot in a direct line ahead of his body, not out to one side, which is more characteristic of bursitis in the shoulder or check ligament lameness. Navicular disease can affect either one or both front feet. I have never seen true navicular disease in the back feet.

Navicular disease may be confused with founder. However, a horse with navicular disease is not anchored to the ground. He does not mind backing up. If the digital nerves to the

227

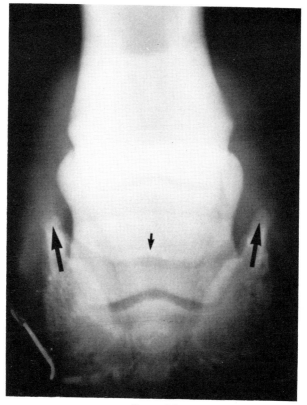

Figure 86

navicular bone are blocked, the horse will be sound and show no evidence of pain. Remember, *the horse with navicular disease walks toe-heel, whereas the horse with founder walks heel-toe.*

One of the early signs of navicular disease is that the horse will dig a hole in a dirt floor and then stand with his toes down in the hole and his heels up on the edge. Some horses will paw straw into a pile and will use this to get their heels up in order to relieve the pressure on the navicular bone.

Navicular disease occurs in all breeds; however, the hoof that is presently on the quarter horse seems to lend itself to this problem. Often there is not enough foot or cushion between the navicular area and the ground. The Thoroughbred and Standardbred, with the straighter wall and higher heel, have more cushion.

A fractured navicular bone or calcification of the ligaments to the navicular bone will produce the same symptoms as does notching of that bone.

Navicular disease usually occurs in older horses, but I have seen it in 3-year-olds.

Butazolidin (Geigy) will relieve the symptoms by reducing the inflammation. In early cases a small dose of steroid injected into the bursa relieves the inflammation so that the animal will show no symptoms. However, as the disease progresses, it is necessary in most cases to remove part of the digital nerves at the level of the pastern.

Some horse owners prefer to have a rolled toe on the shoe

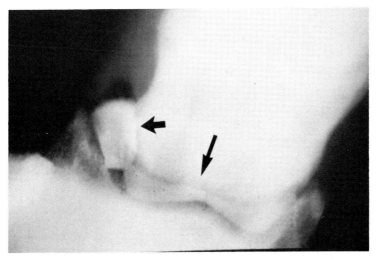

Figure 87

of a horse with navicular disease. A *rolled toe* is a half round shoe sitting back from the end of the foot so that the animal more or less rocks over rather than breaks over a square surface.

Some horses are more comfortable if you can give them a little more heel and leave as much frog as possible for a cushion. Some horse owners square the toe because they feel that the horse breaks over more easily and therefore does not put pressure on the navicular bone.

Nerving the horse (cutting the digital nerves) is usually effective for about a year. The nerve will then form a small neuroma (a ball of nerve tissue) because of the body's attempt to join the two ends of the nerve. This gives the horse a phantom limb syndrome (the animal will feel something that is not really there). Treatment is simply to reoperate and remove the neuroma. This can be done yearly; in fact, I have personally done this seven times on one horse.

Nerving is best conducted under a general anesthetic because the surgery should be carried out under sterile conditions. However, most horses are nerved in the shed row at the race track. One of the mistakes sometimes made when nerving is the removal of the ligament to the ergot, which lies directly over the nerve; thus, the nerve is left intact. The ligament to the ergot is pearly white and flat. It is always a good policy to remove this before nerving.

The nerve is rounded and always has a small blood vessel (*arrow*) running along its edge (Fig. 89). It is yellowish white in color.

As shown in Figure 90, always examine the nerve end for nerve bundles.

When a neuroma must be removed, do not take out any excess nerve (Fig. 91). You may have to go back into the leg next year, and there may be insufficient nerve remaining.

Figure 92 offers a close-up view of a neuroma. *A* is the enlarged end, and *B* is the normal nerve.

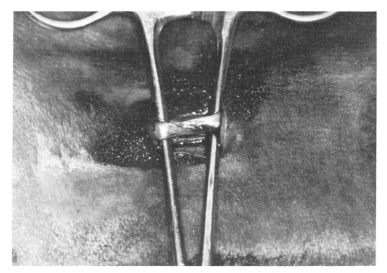

Figure 88

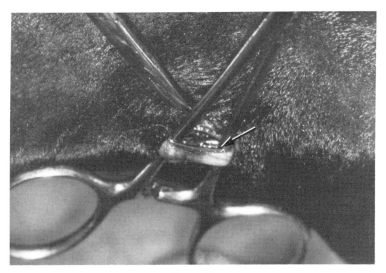

Figure 89

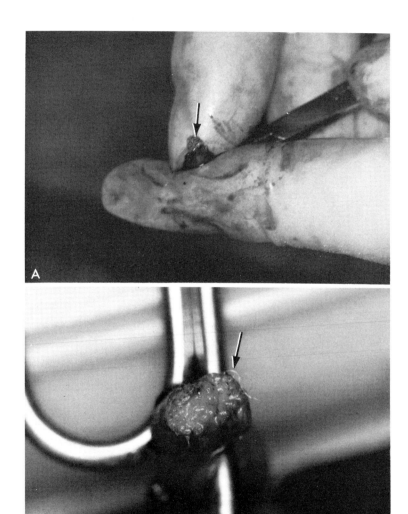

Figure 90

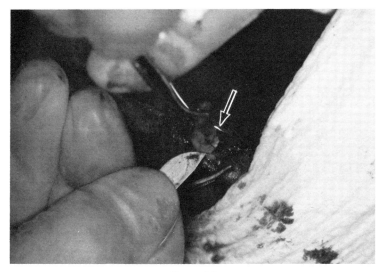

Figure 91

The horse in Figure 93 nerved himself on a fence when he was young, and a neuroma formed under the scar. This animal should be nerved immediately above the scar.

Recent study has shown that if the nerve trunk is cut shorter than the nerve sheath, and the sheath is crushed over the nerve stump, neuromas are not as likely to form.

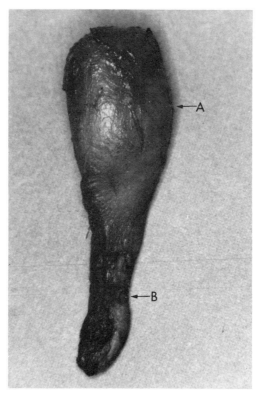

Figure 92

Figure 93

PEDAL (COFFIN) OSTITIS

Pedal ostitis is best described as arthritis of the pedal or coffin bone and is primarily a front foot lameness. It is seen in all breeds of horses and ponies in England and to a lesser degree in North America. It is not very common in Thoroughbreds, but it is common in show jumpers, hunters, and polo ponies. When it does occur in the Thoroughbred, it is often associated with an animal that has poor bone development. The animal that tends to get splints and bone spavins is also prone to pedal ostitis.

Pedal ostitis is probably due to wear and tear, abuse, and foot conformation, and seems to be prevalent in animals with heavy bodies and small feet. It may also be due to poor shoeing and improper mineral balance in the soil.

This arthritic condition comes on very gradually. The first sign is that the horse loses his action—he becomes very short striding in front. Quite often the owner of the horse will not even notice the change because it comes on so slowly.

Pedal ostitis is confirmed by nerve block and x-ray. If the digital nerves (these are the same nerves that are blocked to diagnose navicular disease) are blocked, the horse will become partially sound. X-rays will show that the lateral cartilages have turned into bone and that the bottom of the coffin bone has become pitted. If the nerves to the front of the foot are blocked, the animal will become temporarily sound.

Pedal ostitis is often seen in association with corns. It may be that pedal ostitis tends to occur because of bad shoeing and subsequent bruising of the heels, which in turn cause the coffin bone to become bruised. Without the aid of x-rays it is difficult to differentiate this condition from sidebone formation.

One partial treatment is to nerve the animal by cutting the digital nerves, as is done in navicular disease. Another solution is to cut a groove about a quarter of an inch from the coronet band all around the hoof wall. This groove is cut down to the lamina, thus separating the coronet band from the hoof wall. When the new hoof wall grows down, it will mushroom out and in this way adapt itself to the enlarged coffin bone. This relieves the pressure, and the horse becomes workable again. (Normally, pedal ostitis, when not corrected, becomes worse with work.)

PUNCTURE WOUNDS

Puncture wounds may be caused by horseshoe nails being driven into the wrong part of the foot or by an animal accidentally stepping on a nail.

The foot becomes hot, and the animal is not able to walk on it. When you start trimming around all the nail holes, you will likely notice that the nail is in the sole. If you keep trimming, you will find a grayish white pus that is quite watery. Once you relieve the pressure, the horse will become sound.

Any good poultice material is specific for puncture wounds. Put the poultice into a plastic bag and then pull the bag over the horse's foot. Wrap a heavy cloth or tape around the foot so that it does not cut through the plastic (Fig. 94). The wounds will drain and clean out well.

Remember, *puncture wounds are the most common means by which tetanus germs may enter and infect a horse.* The affected horse should have a tetanus antitoxin or a tetanus toxoid booster shot. It is very important that all horses be vaccinated against tetanus with a yearly booster shot.

The treatment for a puncture wound should be followed up by giving the animal a large dose of an antibiotic such as penicillin-streptomycin. Twenty ml per day for three days should be sufficient.

238

Figure 94

FRACTURED COFFIN BONE

If a horse pulls up and will not put his foot on the ground, it probably means that he has fractured his coffin bone. This is a front foot problem; I have never seen a fractured coffin bone in a hind foot.

To be absolutely sure that a fractured coffin bone is the problem, the foot must be blocked and then x-rayed (Fig. 95). If the fractured segment is large enough to hold a bone screw, surgery is recommended. The animal is put on the operating table under a general anesthetic. In order to provide access to the fracture site, a trefine is used to remove a section of the hoof wall over the fracture site (Fig. 96). The hole made by the trefine is shown in Figure 97. The section of wall that is remqved is put into a warm saline solution until the surgery is completed.

When access to the fracture site has been achieved, a hole is drilled through the fracture (Figs. 98 and 99), and a Vitallium screw is inserted (Figs. 100 and 101). Once the screw is in place, the section of hoof wall is reinserted in the hoof and a cast is applied (Figs. 102 and 103).

The screw prevents the segment from moving, and, as a result, healing occurs much faster.

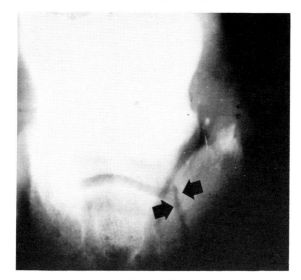

Figure 95

Figure 96

Figure 97

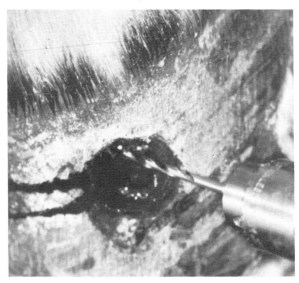

Figure 98

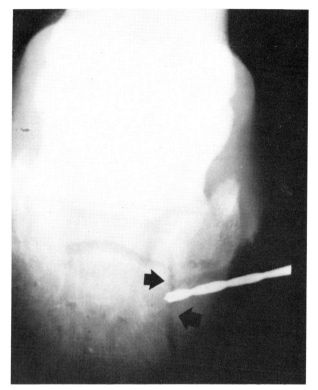

Figure 99

This surgical technique is highly recommended because of the short lay-up time for the animal. Healing time varies with each horse but ranges between three and six months.

If there is any evidence of bone necrosis (demineralization) at the head of the screw when the bone has healed, the screw should be removed using the same technique.

Figure 100

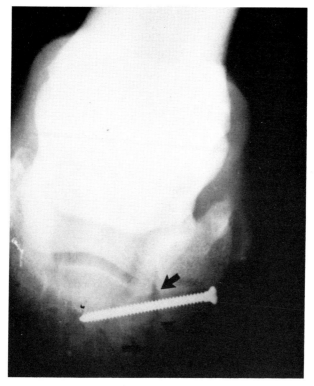

Figure 101

Figure 102

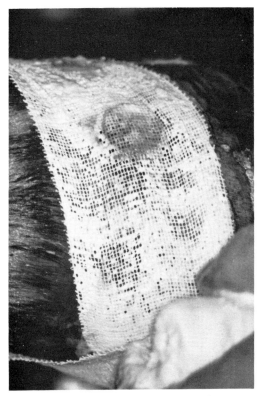

Figure 103

FRACTURE OF THE COFFIN BONE AT THE ATTACHMENT OF THE EXTENSOR TENDON

This type of fracture is quite common. Horses with this kind of fracture are lame even at a walk. Because of swelling of the coronet band in front, this condition is often confused with a stone working through the foot.

With rest, an affected animal will become sound temporarily; however, once he is put back to work he will again go lame. An x-ray of the side of the foot will show a piece of fractured coffin bone that may be as small as a pea or as large as a walnut (Fig. 104).

Treatment is to remove this piece of bone. This is done by making an incision down the front of the pastern to the coronet band; however, the coronet band itself should not be cut. The extensor tendon is then split and separated, and the small piece of bone will be exposed.

Most horses become sound once this piece of bone is removed.

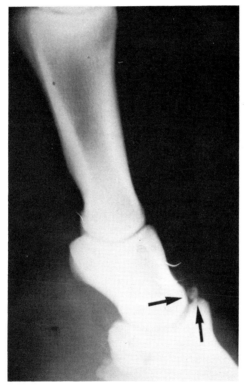

Figure 104

SEPARATION IN THE WALL

Separation in the wall (Fig. 105) is usually initiated by a stone that starts at the white line where the sole meets the hoof wall on the bottom of the foot. The stone works its way up and comes through at the coronet band.

As the stone moves along it causes an infection. An x-ray of the foot will indicate a dark streak, which means that the wall has separated from the coffin bone.

Treatment consists of removing part of the separated wall. Grooves are made in the hoof for this purpose (Figs. 106 and 107). Allow the lamina to dry and then replace the wall with an acrylic or a patch of some type.

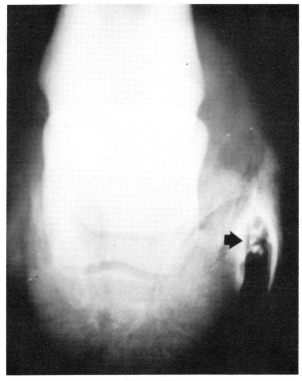

Figure 105

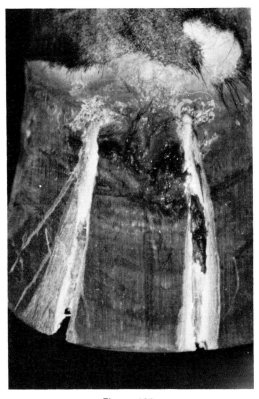

Figure 106

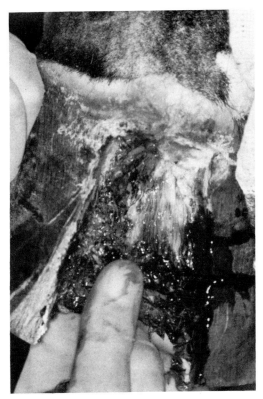

Figure 107

CORONET BAND INJURIES

Usually, if the coronet band is severely injured and the periople (the part of the hoof that becomes white when the foot is soaked in water) is damaged to a great extent, a ridge will grow down the hoof for the rest of the animal's life.

Occasionally, when the coronet band is injured, proud flesh will grow into the area. This proud flesh must be cut out once the base has filled in. Small pinch grafts are then taken from another part of the body, generally the chest, and transplanted to this area (see Skin graft, pages 199–202). The hide will then grow back.

SIDEBONE

Sidebone, which should not be confused with *ringbone* (see page 261), is a calcification of the cartilage that attaches the wall of the hoof to the coffin bone. As a horse grows older, this cartilage slowly turns into bone. A bony outgrowth builds on top of this. Figure 108 demonstrates an extreme case of sidebones. The arrows indicate growth. In this case the side-bones are about an inch longer than normal. I have seen outgrowths as high as 2 inches above the hoof head on old street horses.

Sidebone is diagnosed by blocking the nerves to that area so that the horse will become sound. X-rays are excellent for con-firming this problem.

The cartilage at the coronet band near the heel should be soft and pliable. When this cartilage becomes hard, it is re-sponsible for a great deal of foot lameness.

If your horse is developing sidebones, be sure that the walls do not contract (draw together). If the wall contracts, the sidebones press on the pastern. To widen the heel, emery the foot side of the shoe to the outside. Thus, when the foot meets the ground, the heel will tend to slide sideways off the shoe. This spreads the foot.

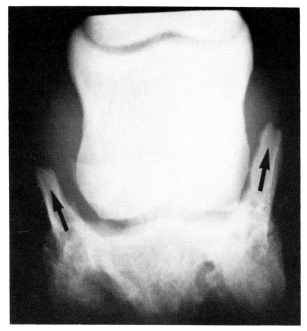

Figure 108

Do not use a bar or clips because these will not allow the foot to slide sideways. Once the foot has spread, an ordinary shoe can be used.

FRACTURED SIDEBONE (QUITTOR)

After a fracture has occurred, the segmented fragment becomes a foreign body and will produce a constant discharge at the coronet band. The problem can be easily diagnosed by x-ray.

The best treatment is to remove the cartilage chip surgically.

BONE, JOINT, AND LIGAMENT PROBLEMS

RINGBONE

When a bone injury occurs, the body sends calcium deposits to the site of the injury. If the injury occurs at a joint, a ring of bone develops around the joint—hence, the term *ringbone.*

Ringbone is an arthritic syndrome that affects the junction of the P1–P2, the pastern joint. At this location it is called a *high ringbone* (Fig. 109). *Low ringbone* at the coronet band involves the P2–P3.

Ringbone starts as a bony growth above and below the joint. Later, it directly involves the joint, which becomes arthritic. The ligaments are then affected, and the animal becomes very lame. Occasionally, a horse will have a small ringbone and never show lameness.

Ringbone sometimes appears in all four legs in force-fed yearlings. This will correct itself, however, if the animal is given a balanced diet and proper exercise.

Ringbone is usually caused by either external injury or internal irritation due to concussion or strain on a particular part of a bone. The animal experiences inflammation and extreme pain. A large, hard swelling occurs on one side or it may go all the way around the leg. Swelling is more common in the front legs but occasionally does appear in the back legs.

261

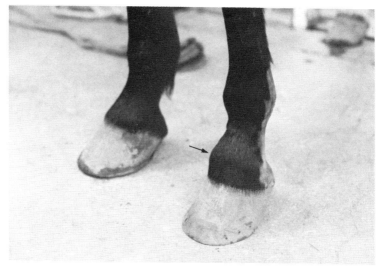

Figure 109

Figures 110 to 114 demonstrate a few treatment techniques. In Figure 110 the arrows indicate the calcium formation (exostosis). A drill is in place to remove the cartilage. A hole is drilled through the P1 into the P2 (Fig. 111), and three vitallium screws are inserted (Fig. 112). Figure 113 shows that the P1 has healed successfully to the P2. The curved arrows indicate extreme exostosis. This exostosis is important because it binds the two bones together. Horses that have undergone this treatment can be successfully worked or raced.

Another procedure that may be followed in treatment of ringbone is to remove the cartilage in the joint with a drill and implant a direct current generator in the leg (Fig. 114). A hole is drilled into the P2 and the anode is put into the bone. The generator (*arrow*), powered by a hearing aid battery, is implanted under the skin at about the middle of the P1. The electrical current encourages calcium to bridge the joint. This apparatus is Teflon coated to prevent rejection.

In addition to the methods of treatment just mentioned, I am now following a surgical procedure that locks the joint. This involves taking some cancellous (reproductive) bone from the hip and transferring it to the open leg joint. Screws are then inserted obliquely across the joint to fix it in position.

Following this treatment, the animal is able to walk on the leg with only a slight amount of soreness. After six months, the first and second phalanges will have fused together and the animal will be ready for training.

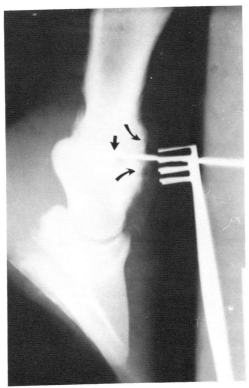

Figure 110

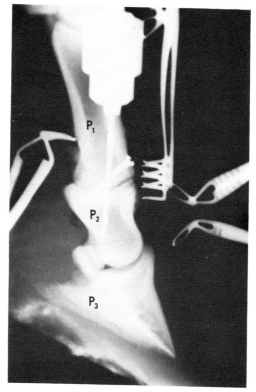

Figure 111

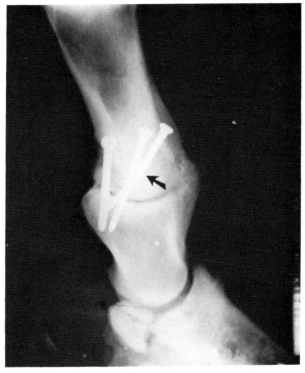

Figure 112

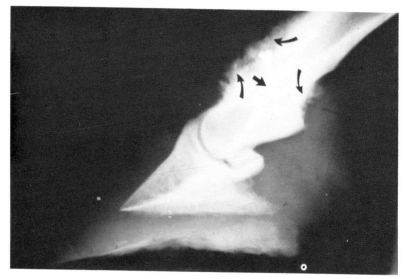

Figure 113

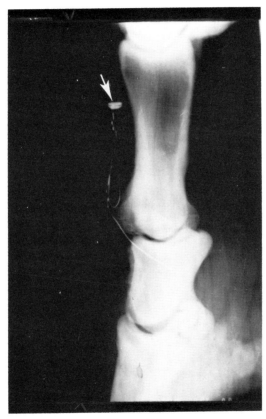

Figure 114

SESAMOIDITIS AND FRACTURED SESAMOID BONES

The horse has two proximal sesamoid bones on each leg. (See Figure 115. A—canon bone; B—splint bone; C—sesamoid bone; D—P1; E—P2; F—P3.) The sesamoids are small, pyramid-shaped bones that sit on the posterior aspect of the fetlock joint. They keep the tendon in place as it passes over the back of the fetlock.

In the embryo the sesamoid bones are formed in the tendon. As the foal grows, the sesamoid bones are enveloped by the joint capsule of the fetlock. They are not weight-bearing bones; however, they are the center of the hinge mechanism of the fetlock. This is the main area of lameness in all four legs.

The main symptom of sesamoid problems is what is called *three-legged lameness* (the animal walks on three legs) with or without swelling. On the day the fracture occurs, there most likely will be no swelling. If the animal is allowed to rest for three or four weeks and then put back to work, the swelling will be obvious.

To diagnose this problem the foot should be blocked with a suitable local anesthetic. Then, each side of the ankle just above the sesamoid bones should be blocked. If the horse

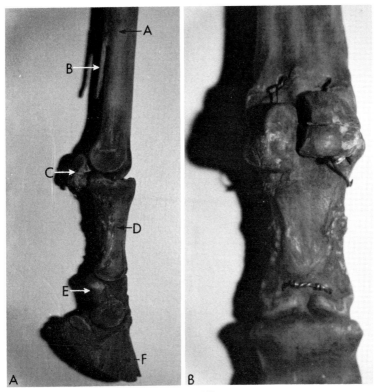

Figure 115

becomes sound at this point, you can be sure the animal has sesamoid problems. An x-ray is the best method of determining whether or not the horse has a problem in this area.

The most common lameness related to the sesamoid bones is called *sesamoiditis* (Fig. 116). The bones become notched owing to demineralization (*arrow*). The notching, which can be seen on x-rays, results in tenderness of the suspensory ligament as it hooks onto the side of the sesamoid bone. This condition is seen most often in heavy, fit animals. I believe it is due to a calcium-phosphorus imbalance; consequently there is

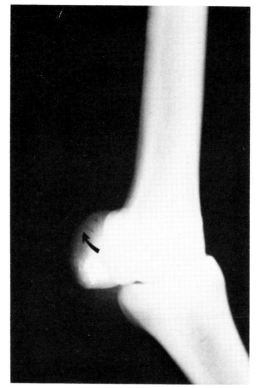

Figure 116

pitting of the bone. Treatment with Butazolidin is beneficial, but cure is doubtful.

The next most common problem causing lameness is the small tip fracture of the sesamoid bone (Fig. 117). This can be easily removed, however. Figure 118 offers a view of the fractured bone inside the leg. The forceps are touching the piece of bone that has broken off from the sesamoid bone. A is the chip; B is the balance of the sesamoid bone. An old tip fracture of a sesamoid bone is shown in Figure 119. Note the calcium

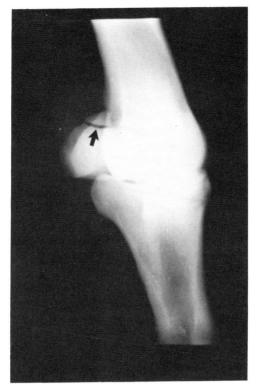

Figure 117

formation as a result of not removing the tip shortly after the fracture occurred. Treatment is to remove surgically the tip plus the calcium. The arrows in Figure 119 indicate the bone and calcium that must be removed. Prognosis is good. Multiple fractures of the apex of the sesamoid (*arrows*) can be seen in Figure 120. This is how the surgeon sees it.

The midline fracture is the third most common problem involving the sesamoid bones. In Figure 121, the dark line between the arrows is a midline fracture. Provided that the two

Text continues on page 276

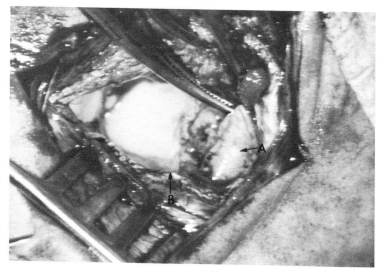

Figure 118

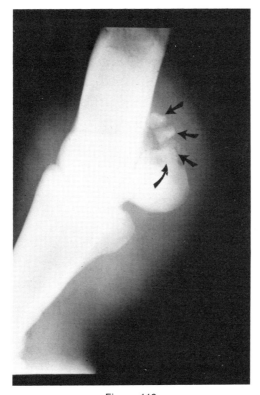

Figure 119

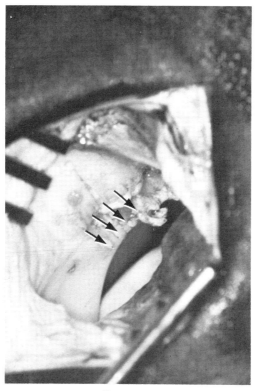

Figure 120

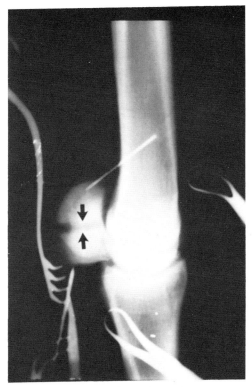

Figure 121

pieces are not too far apart, the sesamoid fragments can be drawn together with a screwnail (Fig. 122).

In the case of a base fracture (Fig. 123), if the segment is large enough to hold a screwnail, the animal will recover (Fig. 124). Note in Figure 124 that some calcium has formed over the head of the screw, but it does not interfere with the locomotion of the horse.

Occasionally, I will find a thin slab fracture off the outside edge of the sesamoid bone where the suspensory ligament is

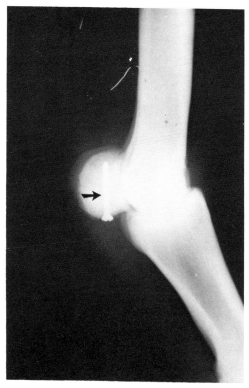

Figure 122

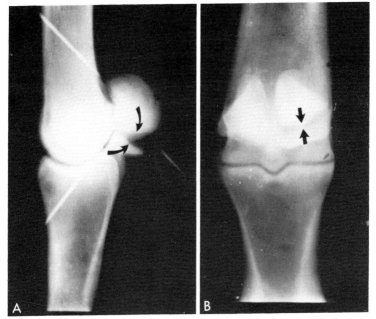

Figure 123

attached (Fig. 125). Using a screwnail to attach this slab to the main part of the bone has not proved very successful. Instead, I find it best to remove the slab and later fire the area to encourage the formation of a scar to hold the suspensory ligament to the bone. Figure 126 shows the pattern used for firing an ankle.

Sesamoid fractures in the front legs of the horse are thought to be caused by the heel of the foot getting into a hole in the field or track while the animal is at speed. When the body weight of the animal moves forward with the toe pointing upwards, the sesamoid bones lock on the back of the fetlock, thus causing fractures. Most of these fractures involve the medial (inside) sesamoid bones.

I believe that fractures in the back leg occur as a result of kicking, because 90 per cent of the fractures involve the lateral (outside) sesamoid bones.

An old fracture of a sesamoid bone is shown in Figure 127. There is extensive calcium formation in the suspensory ligament (*top arrow*). Degeneration of the balance of the sesamoid bone (*bottom arrow*) is also apparent. Treatment is to remove the calcium surgically. Prognosis is uncertain.

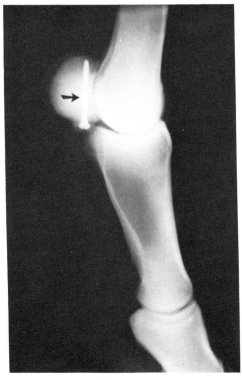

Figure 124

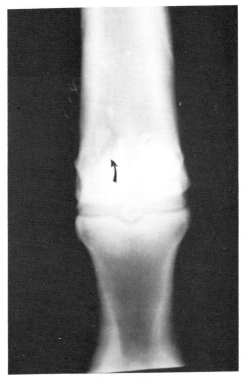

Figure 125

Figure 126

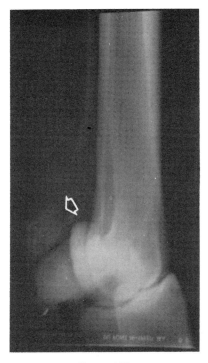

Figure 127

WINDGALL (DISTENTION OF THE DIGITAL SHEATH)

The digital sheath surrounds the ankle and comes down along the tendon. Distention of the sheath is like a bubble about the size of the end of your thumb (Figs. 128 and 129). If you press it, the distention will come up along the side of the ankle. If you massage along the side of the ankle, the ball at the back of the pastern will enlarge.

Some horses tolerate windgalls well and will show no signs of lameness. Others, if the inflammation becomes too great, become quite lame under stress, although they will probably be sound going slow.

Treatment is to draw off the excess fluid (with a needle and pressure; Figs. 130 and 131) and to inject a small amount of steroid with antibiotics into the area. (The dosage is determined by the veterinarian.) This regimen may have to be repeated in about 42 days.

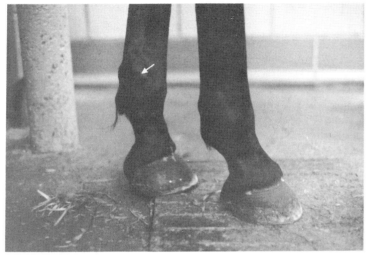

Figure 128

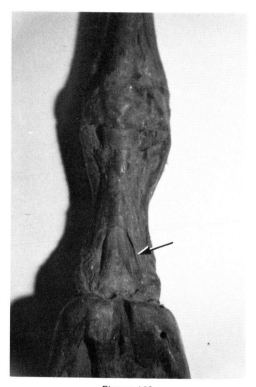

Figure 129

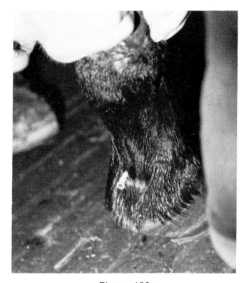

Figure 130

Figure 131

CALCIFICATION SURROUNDING THE P1

Calcification surrounding the P1 is a common problem in the older horse (Fig. 132). Because of injuries, calcium that builds up along the edge of this bone resembles splint material and interferes with the XYV tendons in that area.

Treatment consists of surgical removal in selected cases. In time, this new calcium seems to set and becomes part of the leg.

Many horses are still quite useful in spite of this calcification.

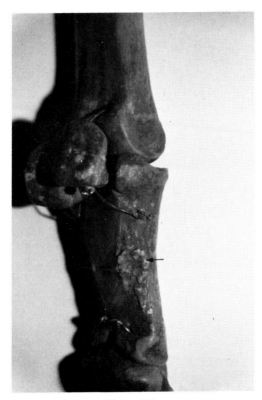

Figure 132

BUCKED SHINS

Bucked shins is a condition that affects the front legs from the knees to the fetlock along the front of the canon bone. A roll usually occurs across the shin.

The periosteum (the membrane that covers the outer surface of the bone) lifts, and inflammation sets in underneath (periostitis). The periostitis may also involve the sheath of the extensor tendon, which is the tendon that picks up the toe, and so the animal may also develop tendinitis.

I see bucked shins most often in the Thoroughbred. Very seldom do I see it in the Standardbred, and only occasionally in the quarter horse. Thoroughbreds usually buck as 2-year-olds, some at 3. Bucked shins are common in horses from western Canada, which leads me to suspect that the condition may have something to do with the calcium-phosphorus ratio in the soil.

Treatment consists of cold compresses and light sweats to reduce the primary inflammation. Painting the skin with dimethyl sulfoxide (DMSO) will occasionally relieve pain. Injection of steroids is sometimes effective in relieving the inflammation, and the periosteum will come back down to the bone again.

Most cases of bucked shins require firing. The skin is clipped, shaved, and blocked (frozen). The shin is pin fired (as in Fig. 126), and a light blister is put on. The horse is allowed to rest for six to eight weeks. The periosteum will then come back down to the canon bone, and, in most cases, this is the end of the bucked shin.

SPLINTS AND FRACTURED SPLINT BONES

A slight rise in the area between the splint bone and the canon bone, anywhere from 2 inches above the ankle to the knee, indicates a splint (Fig. 133). Ninety per cent of most splints are on the inside of the front leg. Five per cent are on the outside of the front leg, and the remaining five per cent occur on the back legs.

Most splints are caused by the tearing of the *interosseous ligament* that connects the *splint bone* to the *canon bone.* Blood clots develop in this tear, and mineral salts such as calcium and phosphorus form in the clot. The lumps that result are hard and feel like solid bone. They seem to appear overnight.

New splints are tender when touched and will cause lameness.

Shin splints may be due to an injury such as being kicked or being hit on the shin, causing a bruise. Blood forms under the periosteum (the membrane that covers the outer surface of the bone), and calcium is deposited in the area of the clot. Consequently, a splint forms.

Splints are not to be confused with fractured splint bones. In the latter case, the fracture occurs first and is followed by a

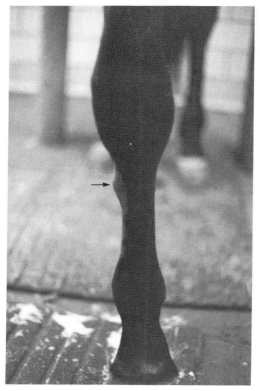

Figure 133

blood clot. The body tries to repair the fracture by sending calcium to the fracture site.

All splints should be x-rayed to be sure that the animal
does not have a fractured splint bone. This differentiation is important because there is usually some *suspensory ligament* in-
volvement with a fractured splint bone.

Most splints are successfully treated by firing and blister-
ing with a light mercury blister. The animal should then have a
few weeks rest. The splint may not disappear; however, it

seems to set, the pain leaves, and the horse becomes useful once again.

If the splint is still soft, it can be injected with an enzyme and steroid; it will then disappear. Some splints can be removed by painting with light irritants such as dimethyl sulfoxide (DMSO), oil of cedarleaf, and iodine. This treatment will relieve the soreness and stop their growth. Once the splints start to recede, the pain leaves.

The splint may also be removed surgically.

Figure 134 shows an old fracture of the shaft of a splint bone. There is a large bony exostosis (*arrows*) as the result of the body trying to heal the fracture. There will be extensive suspensory ligament damage. Treatment is to remove surgically the fractured portion of the splint bone as well as the exostosis. Prognosis is poor.

Figure 135 demonstrates the appearance of a leg with a thickened suspensory ligament due to an old fracture of the shaft of a splint bone with exostosis (as shown in Figure 134).

Figure 136 shows a simple tip fracture of a splint bone. Treatment is to remove the tip surgically. Prognosis is good.

A recent fracture of the shaft of a splint bone is evident in Figure 137. This horse will have a slight thickening of the suspensory ligament. Treatment is to remove surgically the end of the bone. Prognosis is good.

A double fracture of the splint bone that has partially healed is shown in Figure 138. Note the enlargement of the whole bone, which at this stage involves the suspensory ligament. Treatment is to remove all of the enlarged area.

Figure 139 shows part of a splint bone that has been removed. The thickened end is exostosis that involves the suspensory ligament. To show its size, the bone is compared with a Canadian quarter, which is the same size as an American quarter.

Text continues on page 299

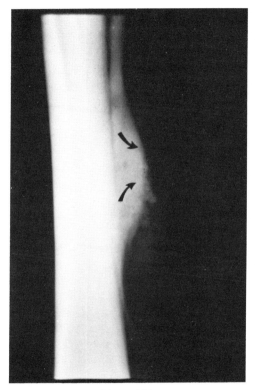

Figure 134

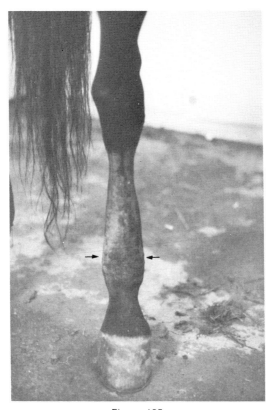

Figure 135

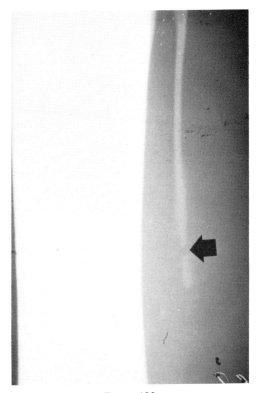

Figure 136

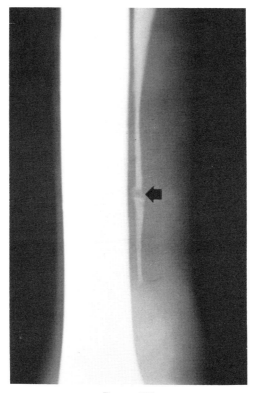

Figure 137

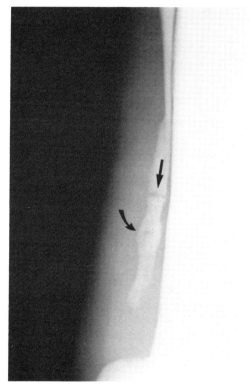

Figure 138

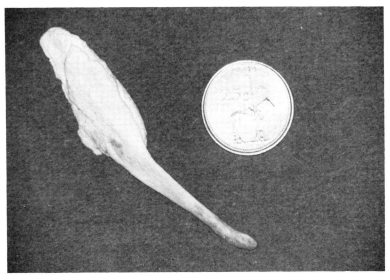

Figure 139

BOWED TENDON

A bowed tendon is an enlargement that occurs on the back part of the front leg from the knee to the ankle (Fig. 140). A high bow is close to the knee. A middle bow is about half way between the knee and the ankle, and a low bow occurs near the ankle.

The two flexor tendons on the front leg (one inside the other) are covered by a tendon sheath. The sheath contains a small amount of oil, which is supplied from the knee and the ankle. This oil permits the tendons to slip freely within the sheaths. When the sheath is ruptured, it cannot contain the oil. Without the proper lubrication the tendons cannot function freely, and the animal loses his ability to move his legs at maximum efficiency.

Because the sheath cannot be repaired naturally, an attempt is made to force the body to make a new one. This is done by firing the leg with a firing iron. The principle behind firing is to bring an increased blood supply to the area. Firing, in a sense, awakens the animal's body to the problem. Firing causes an acute condition, whereas the regenerative processes, when left alone, would proceed slowly. After firing, the small blood vessels in and under the skin pour into the affected

Figure 140

area millions of white blood cells that carry away the damaged tissue and clotted blood.

Ultimately, because of the firing, a thick, smooth, white scar is formed under the skin and around the tendon. This results in a straighter leg because the scar acts as a support. In a sense, this scar serves as a new sheath.

Another way of repairing the bowed tendon is a facial tissue graft transplant. (The horse is a good subject for transplants. Skin punch grafts in large wounds respond well. Cancellous bone chips taken from the hip help bone healing.)

After preparing the animal for surgery, a thin, sharp, pointed knife (tenotome) is used to make several stab wounds in the tendon (Fig. 141). Immediately afterward, sterile dressings are applied and held in place by pressure bandages. The animal is allowed to recover by keeping him in a clean stall for a week to 10 days. He is walked every day, and the dressings are changed every other day.

At the end of this recovery period, the horse is operated on again under a general anesthetic. This time, the leg and the hip

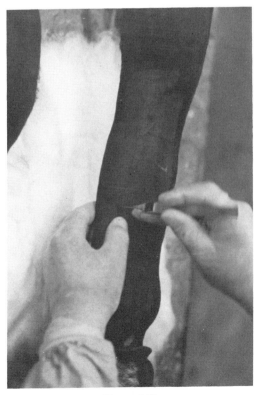

Figure 141

area over the gluteal muscles are prepared for surgery (Fig. 142). A piece of fascia about 16 inches long and 2½ inches wide is stripped from the gluteal muscles (Fig. 143A). A knife with a long handle, somewhat resembling a ½-inch round chisel, is used to form a channel under the skin from the sesamoid bones to behind the knee. The fascial strip is then attached to the knife and pulled down through the channel (Fig. 143B). (Figure 144 shows a piece of fascia emerging from the leg prior to stitching of the incision.) The animal is then stitched, and pressure bandages are applied to keep the sterile dressing in place.

Figures 145 to 149 offer magnified views of sections of tendon tissue. In Figure 145, normal tendon tissue taken from a good leg is presented for the sake of comparison. Figure 146 shows a section of superficial flexor tendon from the bowed leg at the time of surgery, and Figure 147 shows the same section 42 days after surgery. Note the straightening of the collagen

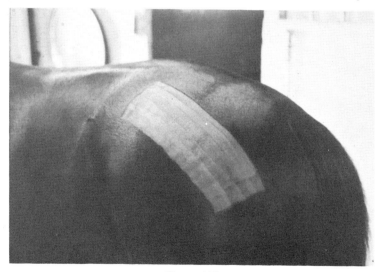

Figure 142

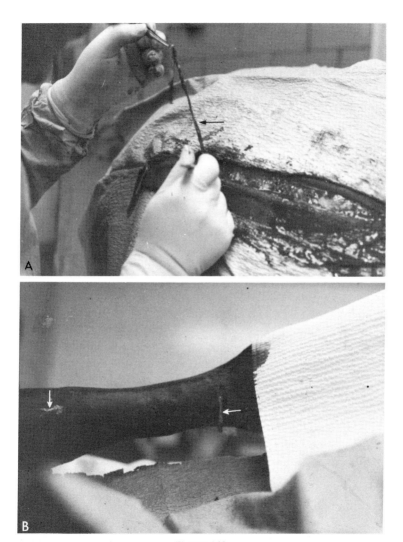

Figure 143

Figure 144

Figure 145

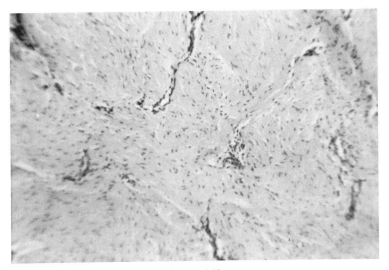

Figure 146

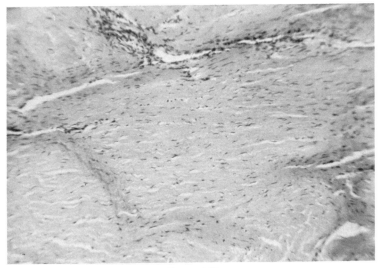

Figure 147

fibers. Old tendon sheath 42 days after surgery is seen in Figure 148, and a fascial strip 42 days after transplant is shown in Figure 149.

After a month, the horse is walked. Two months following surgery, he is allowed to swim in a heated therapy pool. Most horses swim for 15 minutes every day for two months. A mild liniment is applied daily, and at this point, the horse can return to light training. Figure 150 shows the horse four months after surgery. Note that the tendon is somewhat wider from side to side; however, it is straight down the back of the leg.

The deep and superficial flexor tendons are more or less protected by a sheath to a point 3 or 4 inches below the knee. Then, about 2 inches above the ankle the superficial flexor tendon acts as a sheath for the deep flexor tendon. The middle is protected by a thin, fibrous, subcutaneous tissue.

In recent years, corticosteroids have been injected into horses with mildly inflamed tendon tissue. With the support of a cast and with rest, these animals have recovered. More recently fibrolytic enzymes with steroids have been injected into horses with high bows with some success.

Progesterone preparations have been injected into the carpal canal of the horse with a high bow in an attempt to prevent secretion of extra synovial fluid.

Low Bow

The area where the tendons pass over the sesamoid bones and come down the back of the pastern into the foot can become filled with fluid and produce a bowed appearance much like the bows higher on the leg.

There is virtually no helpful treatment for this problem. Allow the animal to rest as much as possible, and perhaps the condition will mend itself naturally. In most cases of low bows the animal remains sound enough to be useful.

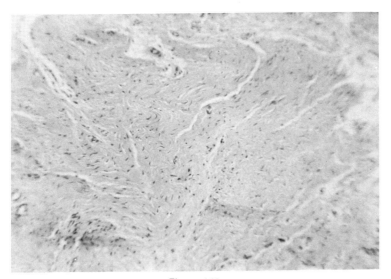

Figure 148

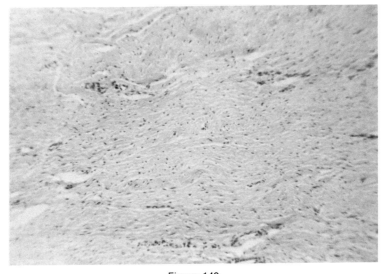

Figure 149

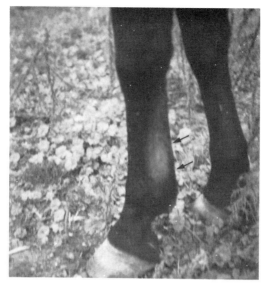

Figure 150

I have found that the digital nerves occasionally become incorporated into the new fibrous tissue that forms in this bow. A pinched nerve effect results. Treatment in this instance is the same as that for navicular disease. The two digital nerves must be amputated below the fetlock.

CHECK LIGAMENT LAMENESS

Front Legs

The top of the check ligament is attached to the back of the knee where the canon bone meets the bottom row of knee bones, and the other end is attached to the inside of the deep flexor tendon, about half way down the tendon. In Figure 151 you can see the superficial flexor tendon (A), the deep flexor tendon (B), and the check ligament in the front leg (C).

Check ligament lameness occurs most often in 2-year-olds, primarily in the horse that is required to draw a load, such as the Standardbred. However, it does occur in other breeds, especially if the animal is calf-kneed. The amount of lameness varies with the amount of ligament that is affected.

If the animal leaves the barn with his front leg out to the side of his body, or walks spraddle-legged, he probably has check ligament lameness. To a certain degree, the animal can warm out of the lameness with exercise.

Figure 152 shows an extreme case of contracted check ligaments. The extensor tendon has become more prominent (A), and the fetlock is flexed ahead (B). In Figure 153, note the box-like appearance of the foot. The angle of the front of the hoof

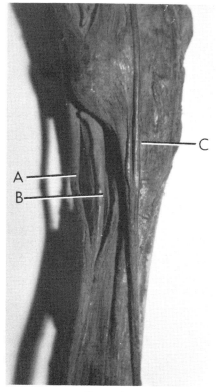

Figure 151

Figure 152

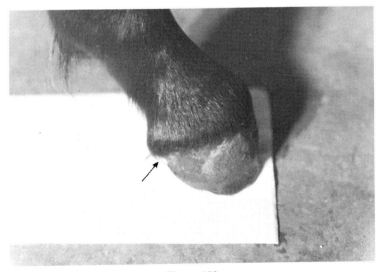

Figure 153

should be in line with the pastern. Treatment is to cut off the check ligament where it joins the deep flexor tendon, about 3 inches below the knee.

The best way to make an accurate diagnosis is to block first the foot, then the ankle, the splint area, and both knee chambers. If the animal is still lame, inject 10 ml of local anesthetic into the check ligament area. If the horse walks off sound, you know that check ligament lameness is the cause of his problem.

In Figure 154, the cutaneous (skin) portion of the superficial branch of the ulnar nerve is frozen. This branch affects the skin over the outside of the knee and the area over the check ligament.

Recommended treatment is to place a few fire holes over the affected area on the outside of the knee and then blister with mercury. The nerve must be blocked before the check ligament is fired (Fig. 155). The animal must be walked every day for six weeks until the firing has healed. He can then be put back into training.

Back Legs

The check ligament in the back leg is a small band of tissue that is attached to the back of the hock and extends to the deep flexor tendon just below the curb area. Figure 156 shows the superficial flexor tendon (*A*), the deep flexor tendon (*B*), the check ligament (*C*), and the splint bone (*D*). When this is torn, the animal seems very lame. There is some swelling.

Treatment is discouraging. Injecting steroids into the area is of some value. Firing is also of some value.

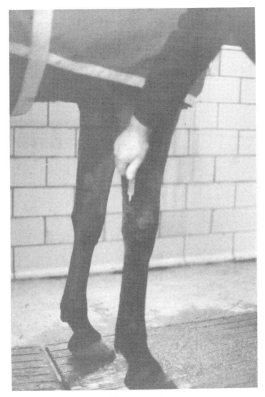

Figure 154

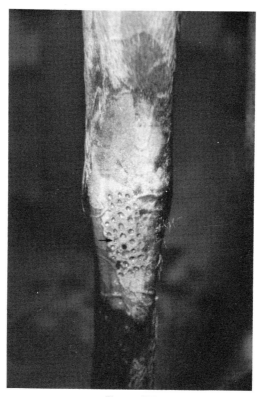

Figure 155

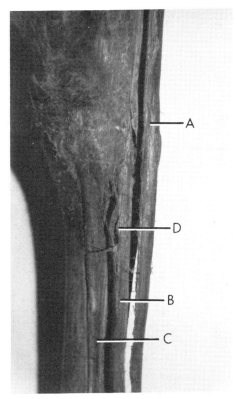

Figure 156

IMMATURITY

The wise trainer will always have the knees of his young horses x-rayed to see if the animals are mature enough to train. Immaturity is indicated by the presence of *epiphyseal carti-lage*—the growing bone in the knee. The epiphysis (growth plate) is completely open from side to side (*arrows*) in Figure 157. This 2-year-old horse would tolerate light jogging. In Figure 158 calcium spurs are starting to form across the epiphysis (*arrows*) in the maturing 2-year-old. The colt could stand light training. Figure 159 shows the knee of a late 2-year-old. The growth plate is almost closed (*arrows*). If this animal is sound, he could work.

I also think it is wise to take x-rays of the stifle at the same time x-rays are made of the knees. It closes in 3-year-olds, but in some 2-year-olds the space is fairly wide and shows that the animal is not mature enough to go into training. Figure 160 shows the stifle of a maturing 2-year-old colt. Arrows indicate the epiphyseal line where the tibial tuberosity joins the tibia. This animal could take light training.

Be careful of the animal whose hips are much higher than

the withers when he is standing on a level floor. He also is probably not mature enough to train.

If you can spot a double fold at the knee, the top fold is at the epiphysis, which should not be visible if the animal is mature.

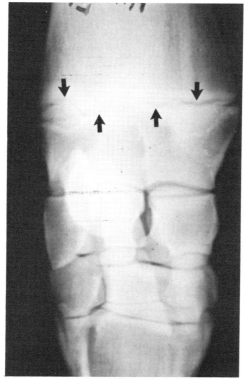

Figure 157

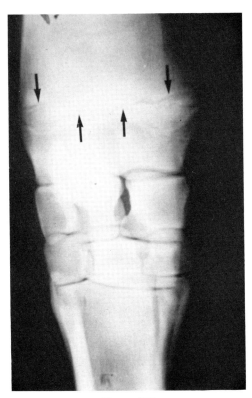

Figure 158

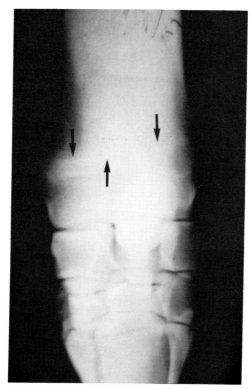

Figure 159

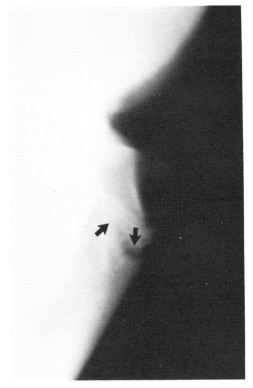

Figure 160

POPPED KNEE

A popped knee is the result of an injury to the knee and is really nothing more than an enlargement of the joint capsule (Fig. 161). The tendency toward popped knees may be an hereditary trait. X-rays reveal no bone chips.

To differentiate between popped knees, knee chips, and arthritis, a hypodermic needle is placed in the joint capsule. In a popped knee, the fluid drawn out by the needle is clear and viscous; in bone chips in the knee, the fluid is bloody; in arthritis, the fluid is thin and straw-colored.

Treatment for a popped knee is to fire and then blister. The knee will then pull into place. As a result of the firing, the pocket that had been formed by the fluid is replaced by a pad of yellow fibrous tissue, and the horse appears normal.

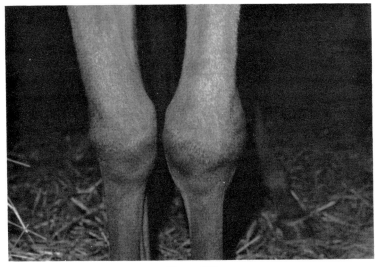

Figure 161

FRACTURED KNEE

Figures 162 to 172 show various types of knee fractures and methods of treatment.

A bone chip of the distal end of the radius (*arrow*) can be seen in Figure 162. The bone chips may be medial or lateral. If the bone chip is small, it should be surgically removed. Figure 163 shows the clipped knee before surgery.

If the bone chip is large enough to accommodate a screw-nail, this is the preferred treatment (Fig. 164).

A slab fracture of the third carpal bone of the knee is shown in Figure 165.

Treatment is to repair surgically with a vitallium screwnail (Fig. 166).

Figure 167 shows a chip fracture at the proximal end of the radial carpal bone of the knee, giving the appearance of a popped knee. It causes an intermittent lameness. Treatment is to remove the chip surgically.

In Figure 168, *A* is normal joint cartilage, and *B* shows raw bone with no cartilage cover. In about 90 days this bone will become covered with a fibrocartilage that serves as a smooth surface and thus prevents pain.

A chip fracture of the distal edge of the radial carpal bone

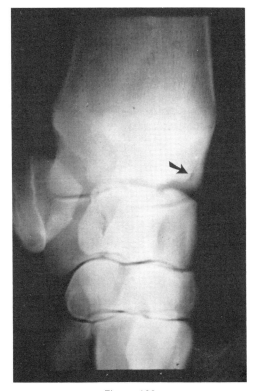

Figure 162

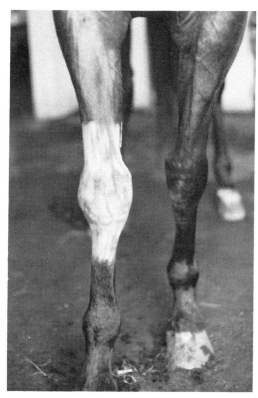

Figure 163

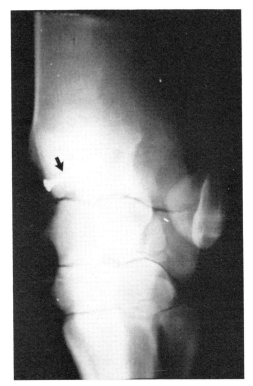

Figure 164

of the knee is shown (*center arrow*) in Figure 169. Treatment is to remove surgically the chip as well as the damaged cartilage on the third carpal bone. Note the piece of calcium in the middle of the radial carpal (*curved arrow*). This should be left alone, as it causes little discomfort. The first carpal bone (*arrow on the right*) may be evident in some horses. This is normal.

Figure 170 shows a large chip fracture of the distal end of the radial carpal bone in the knee. There is also a large calcium projection on the face of the radial carpal bone. Treat-

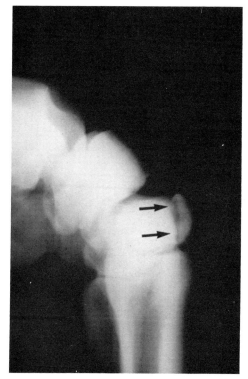

Figure 165

ment is to remove the chip and the damaged cartilage on the third carpal bone. Prognosis is uncertain.

Arthritis of the knee can be seen in Figure 171. In some cases it is beneficial to operate and remove the calcium spurs (*middle arrow*) and damaged cartilage at the junction of the radius and the radial carpal bone of the knee. The other calcium deposits (*top and bottom arrows*) should be left alone. Cases such as this respond well to Butazolidin (2 to 4 grams) given for as long as 30 days. Prognosis is uncertain.

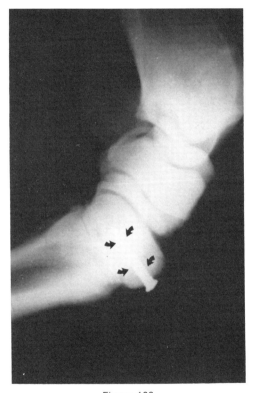

Figure 166

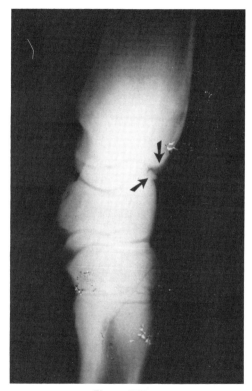

Figure 167

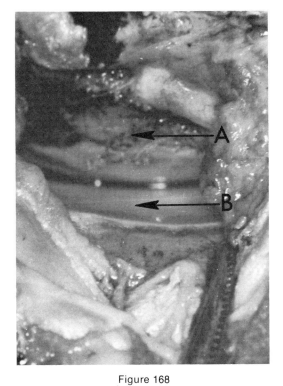

Figure 168

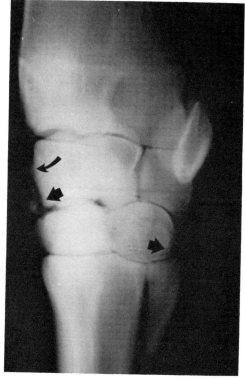

Figure 169

Figure 172 shows a chip fracture and demineralization of the proximal end of the third metacarpal (canon bone). This is where the ligament is attached to the muscle that extends the knee. When removing the chip, care must be taken not to loosen too much of the ligament; otherwise, the animal will not be able to extend his knee. Prognosis is good.

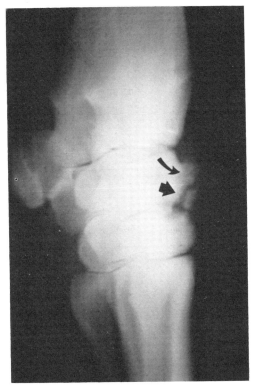

Figure 170

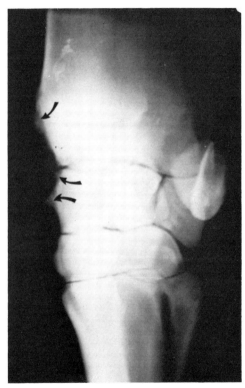

Figure 171

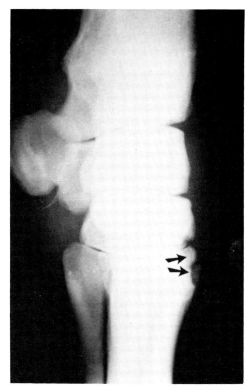

Figure 172

DROPPED ELBOW (RADIAL PARALYSIS)

Dropped elbow is caused by damage to the radial nerve in the shoulder. The radial nerve is the motor nerve for the muscles that bring the leg forward. The degree of nerve damage determines the degree of paralysis. I have seen animals with such extensive nerve damage that they have to drag the leg forward, causing the hair to wear off the top of the hoof head. Others may have only a slight paralysis so that they are able to swing the leg forward and land on the foot.

The radial nerves may be damaged as a result of a trailer accident or the animal running into a gate post or being kicked in the shoulder. A secondary problem that occurs is that the sweeny muscles in the shoulder fall away because of the lack of use.

The animal with radial paralysis is a flat-shouldered horse whose leg hangs from the elbow (Fig. 173). The fetlock rests on the ground. If you pull the foot ahead, the animal will be able to stand on it and look normal until he tries to move away. When he tries to move away, he will not be able to extend the leg in order to stand properly.

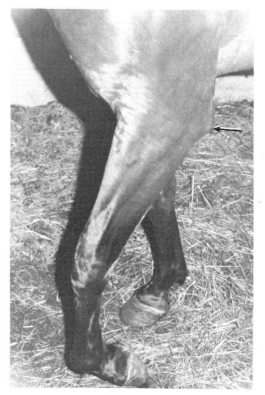

Figure 173

We know that there is very little natural repair of nerves. However, much like a stroke condition in humans, we also know that if there is a will there are ways to exercise the horse in order to regenerate these muscles and make the nerves active again.

I have seen many cases of radial paralysis that have been only temporary. With therapy, the affected legs can become strong, and the animal can be made useful. As soon as the animals can use their legs at all, I swim them. Swimming strengthens their legs, and the horses become useful again.

SHOULDER LAMENESS (BURSITIS)

Shoulder lameness in the horse is very nonspecific; usually, the lameness occurs in the foot. There are two types of primary lameness in the shoulder: Actual arthritis at the point of the shoulder (this is rare), and bursitis of the lateral edge of the shoulder joint.

A small tendon from one of the shoulder muscles passes down and joins at the humerus. Where the tendon passes over the bone there is a bursa that contains a small amount of oil. This bursa can become inflamed. In human terms, this condition is commonly known as *baseball pitcher's bursa.*

The animal affected with this problem points his leg ahead and to the side of his body. The leg points more to the side than ahead. (When the leg points ahead of the body, the problem is usually navicular disease.)

To diagnose bursitis, inject some lidocaine to block the bursa. If the animal walks off sound, the diagnosis is confirmed.

Treatment consists of injecting a steroid into the bursa. This provides temporary relief. Butazolidin (Geigy) also gives temporary relief.

337

SWEENY

Injury to the shoulder area can cause a sweeny. As a result, the muscle at the back of the shoulder area becomes flat. If you cannot determine whether or not the muscle is flat, compare the sweeny to the muscle on the other shoulder, which will be round.

Sweeny used to be a common occurrence in draft horses. Poorly fitting collars can pinch a nerve that comes across the point of the shoulder and cause the muscle at the back of the shoulder to fall flat.

Treatment is to inject counterirritants into the area and, using a syringe, inflate the muscle with air. This stimulates the muscle, and with a bit of exercise it will rejuvenate.

LAMENESS IN THE HIP JOINT

Lameness in the hip joint is rare. When it does occur, however, it is usually the result of a horse spreading both legs out sideways to an extreme degree. Arthritis may develop, or there may be a slight fracture in the pelvis.

I have had few cases of this particular lameness in my practice.

HIP LAMENESS (WHORLBONE LAMENESS, TROCHANTERIC BURSITIS)

A horse with hip lameness almost always points his back foot in a resting position and will be tender over the hips (Fig. 174).

Hip lameness is caused by extreme stress, such as muscle tie-up, or may be due to a slip. Severe cases can be diagnosed by injecting 10 ml of a local anesthetic into the *trochanteric bursa*. This requires the use of a 3½-inch spinal needle.

Counterirritants injected into the trochanteric bursa (whorlbone area) with a 3½-inch needle are the most effective treatment (Fig. 175). MacKay's Injection (MacKay Liniment Co.) and Hypodermin (Haver-Lockhart) are two of the most common products used.

Once a horse has hip lameness, periodic treatment is usually required, but it is quite easily kept under control.

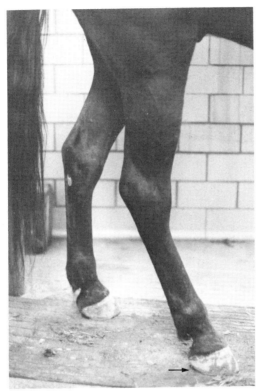

Figure 174

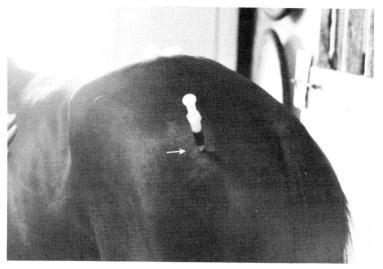

Figure 175

STIFLE LAMENESS

Stifle lameness can be the result of a (1) true arthritis of the joint, with calcium formation on the head of the tibia bone or the head of the femur; (2) poorly placed patella causing friction along the edge of the joint from the patella itself; or (3) short medial ligament of the patella that causes a locked stifle. Each of these causes must be treated differently.

Arthritis of the joint. The prognosis for arthritis in this joint is poor. The joint capsule is distended. When the capsule is punctured with a hypodermic needle, fluid will come out of the needle, showing that there is pressure inside the joint.

Some of these arthritic conditions may be relieved by injecting steroids into the area and keeping the animal on a steady regimen of Butazolidin (Geigy).

Poorly placed patella. The horse with a poorly placed patella that does not lock will invariably knuckle over at the ankle at a slow gait. Since there are three sets of ligaments attached to this bone, all of the ligaments must work in harmony. The animal that knuckles over has too long a medial patella femoral ligament, which runs from the patella to the femur. This allows the patella to ride laterally as the horse moves forward.

Treatment is to inject a counterirritant under this ligament, thus causing a slight swelling under the ligament that takes up the slack. Prognosis is good.

Short medial patella ligament. Should the medial patella-tibial ligament be too short, causing the patella to lock, then this ligament should be severed. This is a very simple operation, and the horse will become sound immediately.

A horse with stifle lameness is more likely to knuckle over if his toes are kept too long. I also believe that a horse with bad stifles should have a high heel. Raising the heel makes the angle of the stifle greater; therefore, the patella fits neatly into the groove. If the heel is low, the hock drops and the angle of the stifle is decreased. When this happens, the patella rides loosely on the front of the joint.

Immature stifles predisposes the 2-year-old to lameness if he is trained too strenuously before the epiphyseal line has closed.

Figures 176 to 185 show cases of stifle lameness due to various causes.

In Figure 176 you can see calcification of the fat in the femoral-tibial joint of the stifle. This causes a severe lameness, which can be diagnosed by placing 10 ml of a local anesthetic into the joint. There is no known treatment.

The arrow in Figure 177 indicates ulceration of the tibial surface.

There is calcium on the femur of the stifle joint in Figure 178. The horse will be very lame, and prognosis is poor. This condition is diagnosed by injecting 10 ml of a local anesthetic into the joint.

There is a large calcium deposit on the femur in the stifle joint in Figure 179. This can be diagnosed by injecting an anesthetic into the joint. This animal is severely lame.

Figures 178 and 179 may be osteochondritis dessicans. However, I have seen this condition when a stifle has been repeatedly injected with long-acting steroids. I have been able to help some horses with this condition by injecting Depo-

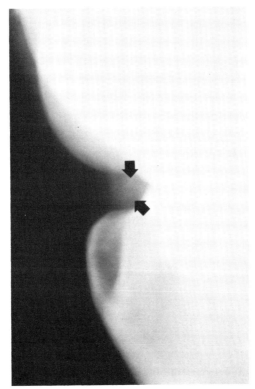

Figure 176

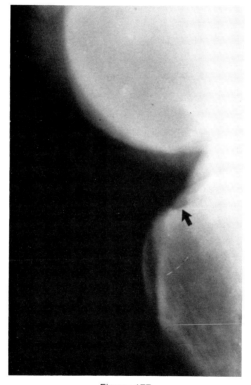

Figure 177

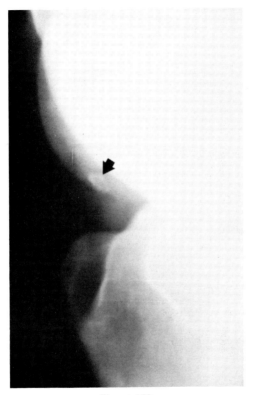

Figure 178

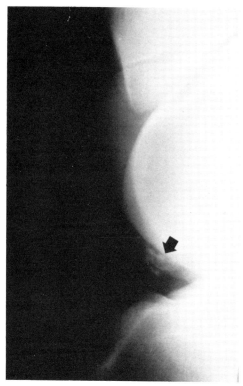

Figure 179

provera (Upjohn) into the joint space. When this drug is injected into the joint, it discourages excessive secretion of synovial fluid.

Figure 180 shows the position of the needle when injecting the counterirritants into the medial patella femoral ligament to prevent knuckling over at the fetlock.

In Figure 181 note the gap (*large arrow*) that indicates that the tibial tuberosity has lifted off the tibia. The gap is a signal that the colt was trained too early. Colts with this condition tend to knuckle over at the fetlock while going slowly. This horse

(Fig. 181) will likely always have stifle trouble. The shadow of the epiphyseal line is evident (*small arrow*).

A mature 2-year-old is shown in Figure 182. Although a shadow of the epiphyseal line can be seen, this colt is mature enough to race or work.

The epiphyseal line is starting to mature in this horse (Fig. 183). Although the lines can be seen from side to side, the center is foggy, indicating that some calcium is starting to form. This colt could take light training.

Figure 184 shows the partially healed epiphyseal line after the tibial tuberosity was pulled as the result of early training. Note the epiphysitis as demonstrated by the calcium spur to the left of the left arrow.

A normal 2-year-old stifle can be seen in Figure 185. The tibial tuberosity (bone above the dark line indicated by the arrows) is not attached to the tibia (bone below the dark line). Therefore, this horse is too young to train.

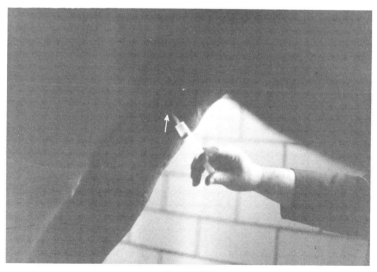

Figure 180

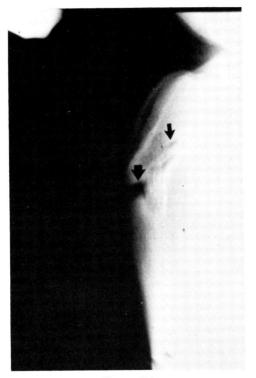

Figure 181

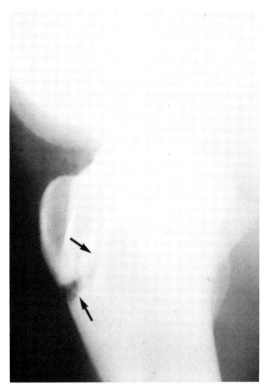

Figure 182

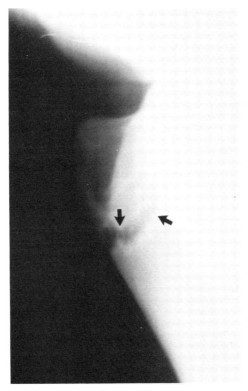

Figure 183

Figure 184

Figure 185

FIBULA BONE LAMENESS

Fibula bone lameness is not a common problem, but it does occur occasionally. The primary symptom is that the horse's back leg swings away from the body as the limb moves forward.

This condition is best diagnosed by x-rays and is usually confirmed only after all other possibilities have been eliminated.

If there is a separation or some arthritic changes, 10 ml of a local anesthetic should be injected into the space between the tibia and the fibula. If the horse travels sound after the injection, one must assume that this is the site of the lameness.

Treatment is to inject 10 ml of 1.9 per cent iodine solution into the area between these two bones.

Figure 186 shows the normal tibia-fibula relationship.

In Figure 187 note the large space between the tibia and the fibula (small bone). This horse has a short fibula, which is common in many animals. Lameness was identified by injecting 10 ml of a local anesthetic into the space (*arrows*). The horse then traveled sound.

Note in Figure 188 the calcium formation at the junction of the tibia and fibula (*short arrows*) indicating the presence of arthritis. Diagnosis and treatment are the same as described for

Figure 187. There are two cleavage lines in the shaft of the fibula (*long arrows*). These are thought to be incomplete ossification centers. Most authorities agree that the incomplete ossification centers do not cause lameness.

Soft tissue calcification associated with fibula lameness is shown in Figure 189. The calcium mass can be palpated near the head of the fibula at the stifle. Treatment is to remove the mass surgically. Prognosis is good.

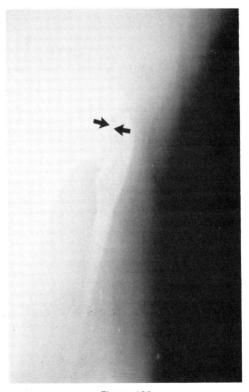

Figure 186

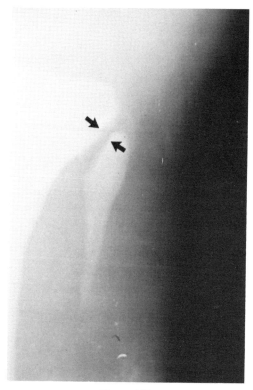

Figure 187

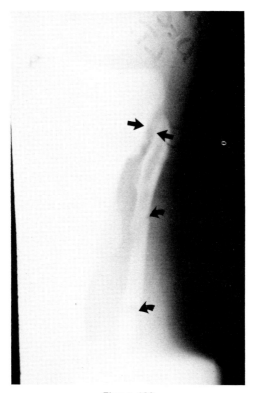

Figure 188

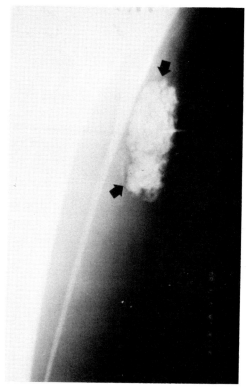

Figure 189

BONE SPAVIN (JACK SPAVIN)

Bone spavin is a calcium deposit on the inside of the hock joint (Figs. 190 to 193). An observant blacksmith can diagnose this condition early because the animal tends to wear out the shoe from the toe to the outside (from 12 o'clock to 3 o'clock) owing to the constant landing on the front outside quarter of his hoof.

The horse rotates the hock away from the body when he first leaves the stall in the morning. In early cases the animal will warm out of the lameness.

One way you can test for bone spavin is to hold the horse's leg up towards his body for two or three minutes. Let it down and quickly move the animal forward a few steps. If he appears to have a cramp in his leg and walks on his toe, you should be suspicious of a jack spavin. X-rays should then be taken to determine the amount of calcium deposit. A local nerve block over the area will also confirm or deny the presence of a bone spavin.

Early cases are treated by simply cutting the *cunean tendon* (Fig. 194) to relieve the pressure. A tenotome (sharp, pointed knife) is used (Fig. 195), and it is necessary to use two motions—down and up—to cut the tendon (Figs. 196 and 197).

Text continues on page 366

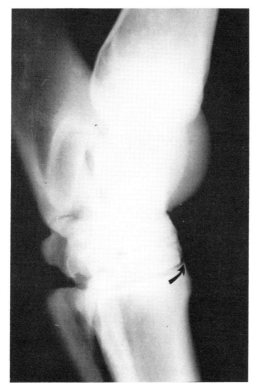

Figure 190

Figure 191

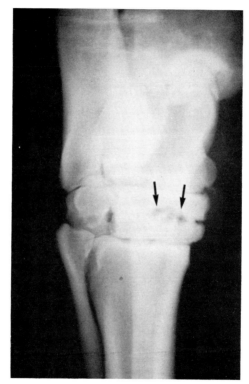

Figure 192

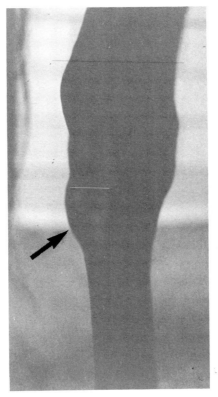

Figure 193

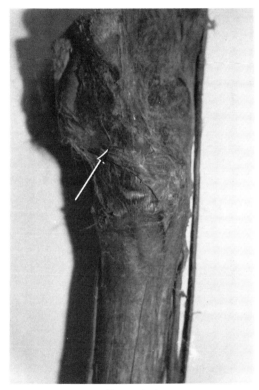

Figure 194

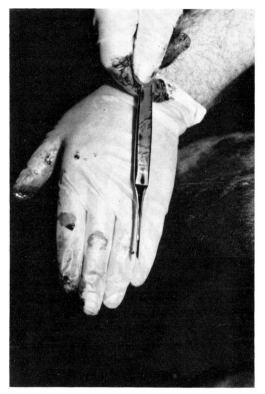

Figure 195

If the cunean tendon is cut on a Monday, the animal can race the following weekend.

Bone spavins seem to run in families in that some stallions tend to throw sickle- or cow-hocked offspring. These kinds of hocks are predisposed to curbs and bone spavins later on. A narrow-based hock is more likely to develop a bone spavin than is a good square hock.

If the bone spavin involves one or all three joint spaces in the hock, the animal has an osteoarthritic condition (Fig. 198). If

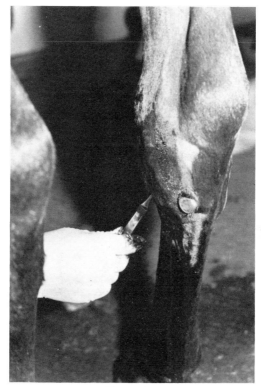

Figure 196

this is the case, becoming sound depends on the bones of the hock growing together. In order to bring this about the animal is put on the operating table under a general anesthetic and is prepared for surgery. I drill through the joint towards the inside of the leg (Fig. 199). Through the same incision I fan out and drill into different areas of the intertarsal joint, thus destroying the cartilage. Once the cartilage has gone, the two bones tend to grow together. Healing time is about four months. The animal can then go into light training.

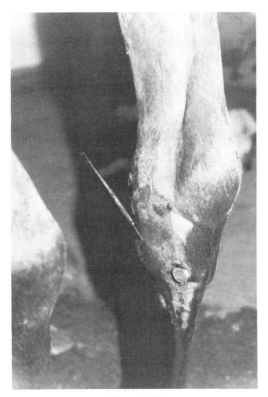

Figure 197

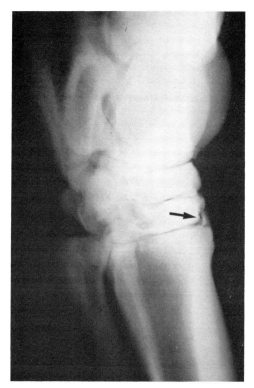

Figure 198

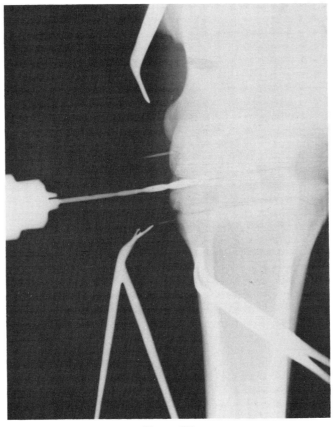

Figure 199

BOG SPAVIN

Bog spavin is a distention of the joint capsule of the hock. The main protrusion is on the inside to the front, immediately above the area of the bone spavin. In most cases it communicates with the thoroughpin (see page 375).

Straight-hocked horses are more prone to bogs than are sickle-hocked horses. The distention is usually about the size of a hen's egg.

As a rule, bogs do not cause lameness unless the fluid is serous- or blood-tinged. Occasionally, they become hot and produce extreme pressure; sometimes they are infected.

Treatment, as in the thoroughpin, is to drain off the excess fluid and inject a drug that discourages secretion, such as Depo-provera (Upjohn), along with a suitable steroid.

Should the bog become infected, inject the joint with an appropriate antibiotic. Massage daily with a light, stimulating liniment, such as tincture of iodine.

CURBS

A curb is a swelling on the back of the hock. It is caused by either a sprained *plantaris ligament* or a torn ligament sheath. A sprain or a tear allows the fluid from around the ligament to get under the skin. As in the bowed tendon, fluid under the skin is foreign to this part of the body, and therefore the body sends white cells into the area. Consequently, swelling occurs.

Curbs can be caused by the horse slipping, with either one or both legs going under the body, or, in the case of a work horse or a drawing pony, by severe strain from a draw.

Curbs are most common in the Standardbred and are frequently found in the Thoroughbred. I personally have never seen them in the quarter horse.

The horse can have what is called a *curby hock*. This is a hock that has too much angle to it. The horse with curby hocks stands with his back legs well under his body. This kind of animal is predisposed to getting a curb as well as a jack spavin. I have seen many horses get curbs as 2-year-olds and jack spavins as 4-year-olds.

An acute curb causes lameness, and the horse tends to walk on his toes behind.

The principle for healing a curb is to establish drainage

and have the tissue heal from the inside out. Therefore, firing a curb is very successful. Firing should not be deep. With the aid of a light blister (Fig. 200) the fluid will seep out through the firing wounds, and the space will be taken up by collagen fibers (scar tissue) as the fluid is excreted.

Some simple curbs can be controlled by injecting an enzyme with a steroid into the area. Occasionally, radium pellets are placed under the hide and apparently dry up the fluid (Fig. 201). The pain ceases once the pressure is removed.

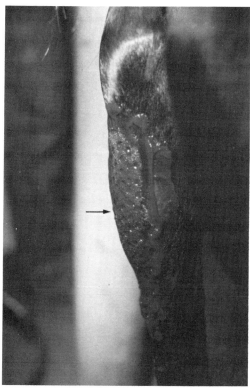

Figure 200

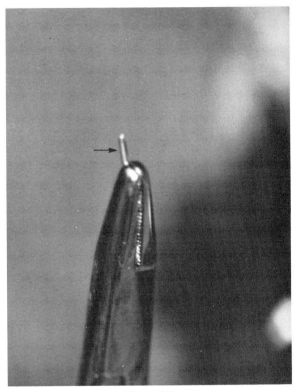

Figure 201

THOROUGHPIN

The thoroughpin is a distention or swelling of the sheath of the deep flexor tendon on the side of the hock and immediately in front of the Achilles tendon. Usually, the thoroughpin and bog spavin are found on the same animal.

The wall of the hock becomes cystic and encourages the formation of extra fluid in the joint. This causes the swelling, which is considered a blemish for show horses, but very seldom does it cause lameness.

Treatment is to discourage secretion. This is one condition in which an interarticular hormone is preferred over a steroid, and the drug of choice is Depo-provera (Upjohn).

After the thoroughpin has been drained, 2.5 ml of Depo-provera will control the problem. This may have to be repeated in 40 days.

Sometimes the hock will be sprained, which will cause blood to accumulate in the joint, complicating the thoroughpin. If this occurs, a suitable steroid should be mixed with the Depo-provera.

CAPPED HOCK

Capped hock is a swelling over the point of the hock (Fig. 202). It may be subcutaneous or may occur between the tendon and the bone.

Subcutaneous capped hocks are easily treated with astringents. I use a product called Diversol (which is made by the Surge Milking Machine Co.). It is used to disinfect the teat cups of the milking machine. When applied twice daily to a capped hock or capped elbow, it serves as a good astringent.

If the capped hock involves the space between the tendon and the bone, aspirate the fluid and inject a suitable enzyme and Depo-provera (Upjohn). Dimethyl sulfoxide (DMSO) is often useful in these cases.

If the horse's problem is a capped elbow, it is advisable to put a bell boot on the foot to prevent the shoe from rubbing the elbow when the animal lies down. House the animal in a stall free of any sharp objects.

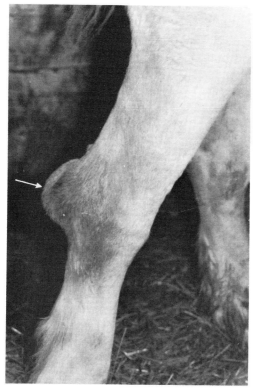

Figure 202

FRACTURES

Most *fractures of the P1* (Fig. 203) heal, irrespective of the degree of the fracture. There may be one fracture dead center, there may be a pie-shaped piece of bone, or there may be multiple fractures.

Horses with fractures of the P1 will become extremely lame, usually while in competition. A front or back leg may be involved. I find that, in most cases, the fracture can be repaired with plaster of paris casts. The horse is put on an operating table under a general anesthetic. A set of blocks and pulleys are applied to the foot in order to get extension so that the pieces of bone can be manipulated back into place without cutting the hide.

Put the first cast on from the hoof head to the knee, or hock, and allow it to dry. Weld a piece of flat steel to the front of the shoe and bend it to the contour of the first cast. Then put another cast over this steel. This distributes the weight from the bottom of the foot to the knee (hock). This also prevents the fetlock from moving and immobilizes the fractured area. *Two pieces of broken bones that are immobilized must heal.*

Recovery is from six months to one year, depending on the type of fracture.

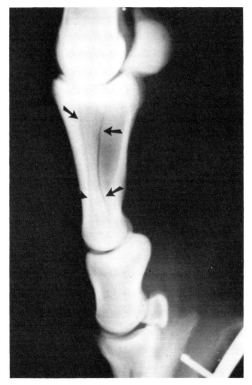

Figure 203

Occasionally the P2 will fracture, (Figs. 204 and 205), but this is rare. The symptoms are the same as those for fracture of the P1 except that the swelling is lower and involves the hoof head, and this fracture can be diagnosed by x-ray.

Immobilization of that area by casts and flat iron welded to the shoe, and time to recover, will permit the animal to once again become a useful horse.

This same principle is used to set a simple *fractured canon bone* (Fig. 206A). With the horse under anesthetic, line up the bone (Fig. 206B). Then immobilize the area by means

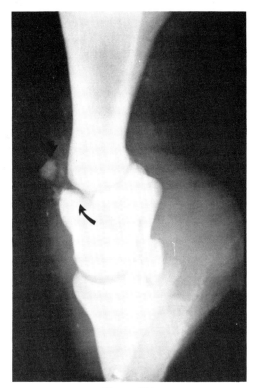

Figure 204

of steel rods and a cast (Fig. 206C and D). Given time, the bone will heal (Fig. 206E).

However, if the fracture is compound, bone fragments lacerate and protrude through the skin; therefore, the bone will not heal well. Infection gets into the bone, and this prevents healing.

I have found that a *fractured femur* is a lost cause. The musculature is too deep to allow effective treatment. If you *can* reach the bone and set it with plates, the animal will spring the plates and pull the pins as soon as he gets up on his feet. The best way to handle this situation is euthanasia.

I have never been able to heal a *fractured humerus.*

Jaw fractures are quite common. Midline fractures occur in foals and are repaired by putting a pin through the bone. Generally, these fractures are caused by being kicked. Jaws heal very well.

Neck fractures usually result in paralysis, and I would recommend euthanasia in these cases.

A *fractured patella* in the stifle can be repaired by being bolted or pinned. The horse may never be perfect, however, because the patella has many ligaments attached to it.

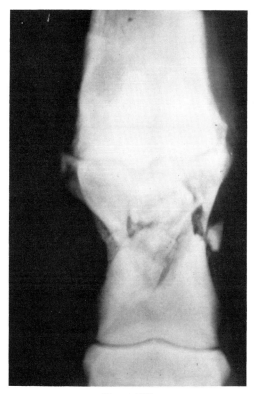

Figure 205

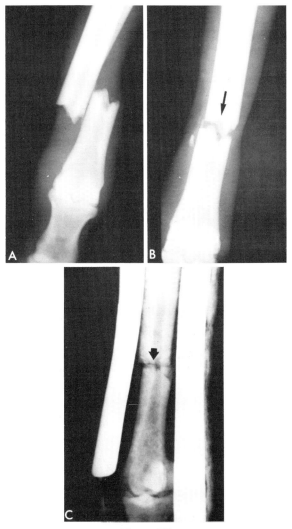

Figure 206

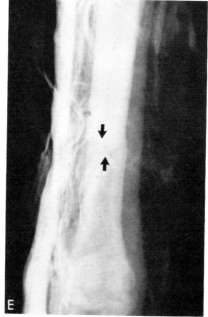

Figure 206 *Continued*

A *fractured pelvis* will heal on its own if the animal is able to get around and if enough healing time is given. If the fracture is bilateral, the horse will be down, and there is no hope that he will live. However, if only one side is broken, the animal will learn to carry that one leg and it will eventually heal.

It is very difficult to set a *fractured radius*. This is the bone between the elbow and the knee in the front leg. If a young animal is involved, and he tolerates a splint, the fracture will heal. However, the older horse presents a difficult problem. To put a cast on this part of the leg is impossible. The animal perspires into the cast, which softens it, and if he wants to get up, he puts weight on the leg, which bends the cast. It is almost an impossibility to get rods, pins, or plates with the strength to hold a horse. If too much metal is used, the body will reject it. Generally, a horse with a broken radius is a case for euthanasia.

Fractures of the scapula, or shoulder blade, usually occur about 2 or 3 inches from the head of the scapula. Some of these heal on their own. I know of a horse that made the International Pace in New York a few years ago that at one time had a fractured scapula. He dragged his leg for months, and it healed on its own. Once the animal started to use his leg again, all the muscles rejuvenated.

Occasionally I see a horse with a slight *fracture in the hock* (Fig. 207). In most cases, I remove the fragment and allow the fracture to heal. Sometimes I must destroy the cartilage of the intertarsal joint to allow the two bones to grow together. Once they fuse, there is no pain. In Figure 208, torn ligaments caused a dislocation in the hock. A cast is used for repair.

Chip fractures to the P1 can occur in front of the ankle (Fig. 209). The chip can be removed surgically by splitting the extensor tendon and manipulating the area to get the chip out. Prognosis with this kind of fracture is good.

However, the chip fracture at the posterior surface of the P1 is hard to treat, since the ligaments are deep through this area

(Fig. 210). If the fragments *can* be reached and removed, the recovery time is about three months.

The horse with a chip fracture at the posterior surface of the P1 will have an intermittent lameness that is often not diagnosed. It seems that this piece of bone moves periodically, causing the intermittent lameness. With rest the animal will become sound, but under stress and work he will become lame.

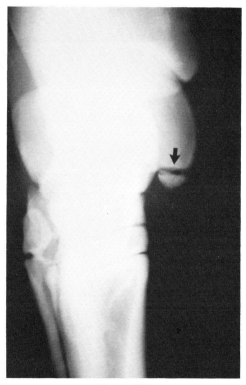

Figure 207

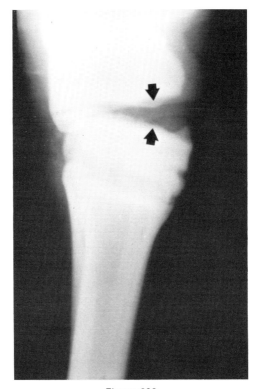

Figure 208

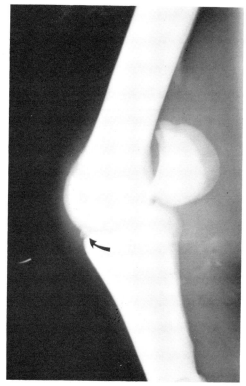

Figure 209

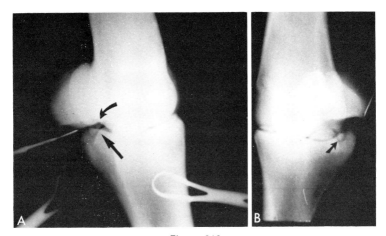

Figure 210

ROACHED BACK

When the horse with a roached back is palpated, the spine will be very tender. The muscles in the back along both sides of the spine will be sore, and when the animal is x-rayed, a fractured spinous process (that part of the spine that forms a ridge along the back) is usually found. The fracture may be only to the cartilage tip of this bone or it may be 2 inches deeper.

Partial fusion of the spine in older animals can cause a roached back, but the fractured spinous process is the most common cause of a roached back in the race or pleasure horse.

Treatment is to remove surgically the loose fragment. This is done by dissecting the muscles away from the spinous process. The fractured bone should then be sawed off square, and the incision sutured.

Prognosis is very good.

SACROILIAC INJURIES

An injury to the sacroiliac area is diagnosed by running your thumb and finger along each side of the animal's spine. If he is sore, he will tend to crouch. The injury is caused by the animal going over backwards and hurting himself.

I find that 2 ml of counterirritants injected on each side of the spine at about five points down the length of the sacroiliac area stimulates circulation and resolves the problem.

SACROILIAC LAMENESS

In some cases of sacroiliac lameness one of the tuber-sacrale of the ilium appears to drop and the muscles shrink away, as in Figure 211. Treatment is to inject 2 ml of counterirritants at about five points down the length of the sacroiliac area.

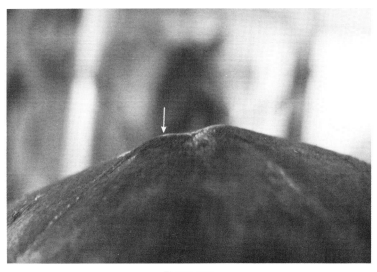

Figure 211

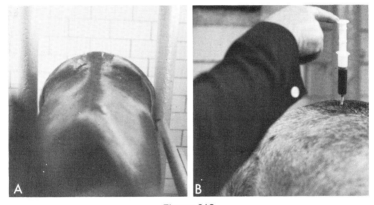

Figure 212

MONDAY MORNING DISEASE (AZOTURIA)

When an animal has had a day or two of rest while on full feed and is then given sudden exercise, a partial muscle spasm or tie-up can result. This spasm is thought to be caused by an abnormal amount of glycogen stored in the muscle tissue. As this glycogen breaks down, one of the by-products is lactic acid. The lactic acid builds up in the muscle and causes a *myositis,* which manifests itself as a partial spasm or tie-up. One of the symptoms of azoturia is coffee-colored urine.

There are many variations of the azoturia complex. A small or large number of muscles can take on this "charlie horse" complex almost immediately after vigorous exercise following a day off while on full feed. At this state, if the azoturia has produced only a slight lameness, the animal may recover by itself if it is put into a stall and kept at rest.

Another variation is that the animal may suffer spasm to his hind end, although he may stay on his feet. He will be completely stiff behind, his muscles will feel like wood, and he will knuckle over if you try to move him. If you can get him back to his stall, he will probably recover in two or three days.

The symptoms of severe azoturia are colic, stiff muscles, and the inability to pass urine. The animal with severe azoturia will go down, and not even a set of slings will allow him to stand.

I believe that the degree of azoturia is in direct proportion to the amount of lactic acid built up in the muscles. The cause of the spasm as well as the lactic acid may not be due entirely to the rapid breakdown of glycogen. It may be due to a lack of proper enzymes and vitamins that convert lactic acid back to glycogen.

Vitamin B_1 is probably the most important of the many catalysts that help convert lactic acid back to glycogen. Injecting vitamin B_1 into the horse before he starts to work will prevent muscle tie-up. It will also treat it.

The co-enzymes in the horse's system are enough to handle any emergency. However, the flavins, such as riboflavin, may be as important as vitamin B_1 in this respect. Horses that fatigue easily are given an abundant amount of flavin so that they will have more stamina.

I conclude from this that azoturia may be due not to too much glycogen stored in the horse's muscles but to a less than adequate amount of the flavins and vitamin B_1 (thiamine hydrochloride) necessary to handle the lactic acid build-up.

Some believe that a diuretic (a drug that increases the flow of urine) also prevents the tie-up syndrome. This belief has proved true in the race horse business. I know that many mares that seem to be predisposed to it are given mild diuretics on a daily basis to prevent tie-up syndrome. This syndrome seems to occur more often in mares than in stallions or geldings.

If your horse gets azoturia, do not work him. Tie him to a tree. Do not try to get him back to the barn, since the more exercise you give him the more muscle will be destroyed. (Coffee-colored urine is a sign that muscle has been destroyed.) Supply him with a sufficient amount of vitamin B_1 and riboflavin to neutralize the lactic acid build-up. Follow this with a therapeutic dose of Lasix (Hoescht-Roussel). (Lasix is a diuretic that produces urination in 10 minutes.)

Once the urine starts to flow, I like to run 2 or 3 liters of electrolytes through the animal. I believe this increases the output from the kidney and consequently eliminates the waste products of the metabolic process.

Should there be enough muscle destruction that the muscles are sore after the animal has recovered from muscle tie-up, injectable vitamin E and selenium should bring him back to normal in a few days. A product called E-Se (Burns Pharmaceutical of California) is recognized as one of the better sources of vitamin E and selenium. Use the dosage recommended by the manufacturer.

I believe that other cases of local azoturia sometimes occur. Large shoulders on a horse that has had to lie a long time on an operating table is considered a localized azoturia.

I also believe that a very mild case of azoturia complex is just straight muscle fatigue. The animal is simply unable to finish his work owing to the build-up of lactic acid. From this I conclude that a racing or working animal should have access to extra B_1 (thiamine hydrochloride) and the riboflavin group.

If the animal is going to have a day off, give him half his normal amount of grain. Bran can be substituted for half his feed. To be sure that the kidneys are working properly, a small amount of diuretic powder can be given that will produce adequate urination without dehydrating the animal.

Grains are high in B_1 and riboflavin, but certain horses are unable to utilize this feed. These horses must be given B_1 (thiamine hydrochloride — 10 ml of 100 mg per ml) by hypodermic periodically so that they will not tie up.

SPECIAL TREATMENT PROCEDURES

CRYOSURGERY

Cryosurgery is a method of treatment that involves freezing of tissue. It is used to remove fibroids, granulomas, tumor masses, unsightly scars, and so on. Figures 213 to 220 show how this technique was used on a mare who had a 1-year-old tumor mass (Fig. 213). The mass started as a weeping wound resulting from the mare being down in her stall for several weeks following abdominal surgery.

In Figure 214 you can see that rubber tubing acts as a tourniquet above the tumor mass. The tumor is excised in chunks to avoid cutting large blood vessels. With the tourniquet still in place, the edges of the wound are cut down below skin level (Fig. 215). A large cryospray unit (made by Brymill Corporation) is used to apply nitrogen gas to the existing base of the tumor (Fig. 216). This reduces the temperature of the tissue to about $-48°$ C, which destroys the cells of the unwanted tissue but has little adverse effect on the surrounding healthy tissue. A special thermometer is used to measure the temperature so that the veterinarian can regulate the amount of freezing (Figs. 217 and 218). As the area thaws, an electric cautery is used to seal the small blood vessels (Fig. 219). The wound is left open to the air, and zinc lotion is applied daily for about four months.

Text continues on page 407

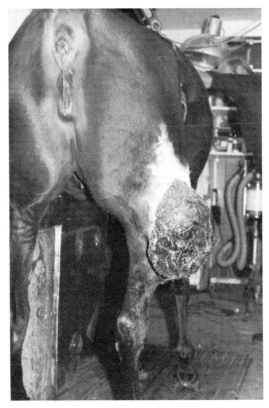

Figure 213

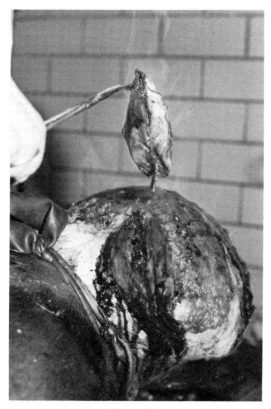

Figure 214

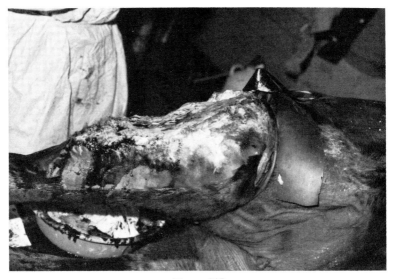

Figure 215

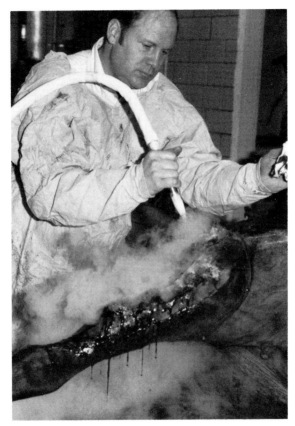

Figure 216

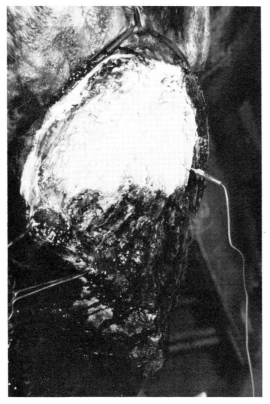

Figure 217

Figure 218

Figure 220 shows the wound six months after cryosurgery. The skin edges are closing in, and the tumor base has stayed below the skin edge. The mare had a normal foal following this surgery and today enjoys good health, although some scar tissue remains.

I have found that vapor coming from the spray unit tends to scare the patient, so I recommend that cryosurgery be done under a general anesthetic.

A disadvantage to this method of treatment is the storing of the liquid nitrogen. It evaporates quickly and is quite costly; however, certain companies or Department of Agriculture units that store frozen semen can be found in most areas of the United States and Canada. They will have a constant supply of liquid nitrogen. The cannisters that we use hold 5 to 10 liters of nitrogen, which lasts about two weeks. The containers must then be refilled.

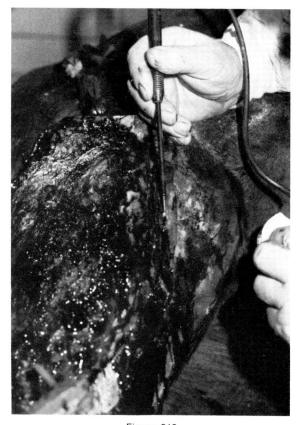

Figure 219

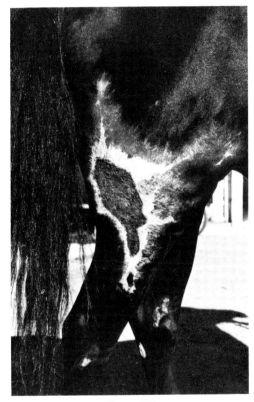

Figure 220

ACUPUNCTURE

Acupuncture is a method of treatment that is popular in Japan and China but at the present time is not used much by western physicians. Although no university or college in North America teaches Chinese acupuncture, certain universities have in recent years held seminars sponsored by the International Acupuncturist Association.

As of 1977 there have been two seminars given: one at the University of Cincinnati and the other at Purdue University, Indiana. There will be another seminar this year in Atlanta, Georgia.

In Taiwan and Japan, acupuncture is regarded in much the same way as we regard first aid. Everyone who practices acupuncture in these two countries, whether a masseuse at a public bath, a judo expert, a physiotherapist in a hospital, or a true acupuncturist in an acupuncture clinic, uses the same system of acupuncture points. Application may vary, but in principle, the system is the same everywhere. For the acupuncture points of the horse, see Figure 221.

According to the Chinese, acupuncture is a system of checks and balances, a system of balancing energy, a system

410

they describe as yin and yang, negative and positive. When either the yin or yang is in excess, the body is very ill.

Acupuncture includes a set of principles. With these principles, one can work out formulas to bring about relief of pain. Often a cure can be gotten simply by moving energy along meridians, which are either positive or negative.

The word *energy* is described in Chinese as *chi*. The chi travels along the meridians. Positive meridians, or yang, run along the back and the outside of the limbs. The yin, or negative meridians, are along the stomach and the inside of the limbs. If energy travels down one limb as yang, it comes back as yin.

This energy is stimulated in several ways: by applying a needle to a designated point, by burning an herb-like material called moxa to create heat on a designated point, by placing direct current electric pads over the acupuncture point on the meridian, or by placing needles in the acupuncture point and then connecting them to a direct current. Sometimes energy can be made to flow simply by massaging the acupuncture point.

The movement of energy can be seen with infrared film. For example, a needle is placed in an acupuncture point near the foot, and a second needle is placed in another point along the same meridian near the elbow. Both needles are then connected to a direct current source, and photographs are taken with infrared film. The pictures will show a great increase in heat.

Acupuncture can become a valuable method in the treatment of horses; however, more literature on the subject is needed. At the present time, several handbooks are available that deal with human acupuncture, and I am sure that in the near future we will be able to consult articles concerning acupuncture for animals.

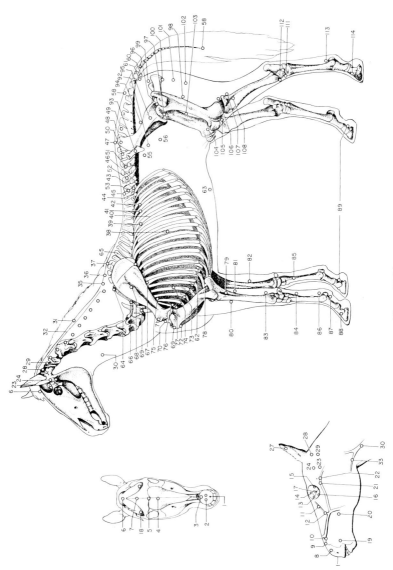

Figure 221

INDEX

Note: In this index page numbers in *italic* indicate illustrations; the preposition "vs." refers to differential diagnosis.